seven questions series

FOREST
AVENUE
PRESS

Brave on the Page

Oregon Writers on Craft
and the Creative Life
edited by Laura Stanfill

First edition 2012

ISBN: 978-0-9882657-0-7

Cover design: Gigi Little
Mount Hood cover photograph by Sarah McDevitt
Typewriter photograph courtesy of Morguefile

Copy edited by Annie Denning Hille and Nancy Townsley

Published in Portland, Oregon, U.S.A.
by Forest Avenue Press
on the Espresso Book Machine
at Powell's Books, 1005 W. Burnside, Portland, OR 97209

www.laurastanfill.com
To order additional copies: www.ondemandbooks.com

Contents

Foreword   vii

interviews

Lauren Kessler: Narrative Nonfiction   11
Yuvi Zalkow: Literary Fiction,
'Failure Conduit'   21
Kim Cooper Findling: Memoir   29
Liz Prato: Stories, Novels, Classes   37
Shasta Kearns Moore: Children's Literature   45
Kristy Athens: Cross-Genre Nonfiction   53
Julia Stoops: Literary Fiction, Art, Web Design   61

Shiny Object, Shiny Object   72
By Kate Gray
Because I Like the Letters   74
By Stevan Allred
Brave on the Page   76
By Kristen Forbes
Why I Write Out Loud   78
By Robert Hill
Where   80
By Liz Scott
Move   82
By Jackie Shannon Hollis
Running Commentary   84
By Nancy Townsley
Add Real Stuff to Your Fiction   86
By Sherri H. Hoffman
Pen and Paper   88
By Steve Denniston
When I Am in My Write Mind   90
By Harold L. Johnson
Fish Lake, Yo   92
By Bart King
Mentor   94
By Gigi Little
Making Feral Creatures   96
By Tammy Lynne Stoner
Pinewood Table   98
By Joanna Rose

flash essays

Wherever I Am   100
  By Emma Burcart
Starbucks and Sensibility: A Love Story   102
  By Nicole Marie Schreiber
Dialogue for Dollhouse People   104
  By Amber Krieger
Overnight   106
  By Laura Stanfill
How I Write   108
  By Kristi Wallace Knight
Sometimes Found-Wisdom
Is Green and Slimy   111
  By S.B. Elliott
Cynicism   113
  By Gina Ochsner
Who   116
  By Mary Milstead
The Call of the Wild   118
  By Martha Ragland
It's All Right to Write and Not Publish   120
  By Brian M. Biggs
What? Me? Well... Maybe!   122
  By Gregg Townsley
Justification   124
  By Dian Greenwood
The Writer as Creator   126
  By Christi Krug

flash essays

Jon Bell: Oregon Nonfiction   131
Scott Sparling: Trains, Drugs and
Literary Fiction   139
Matt Love: Independent Publisher,
Oregon Nonfiction   149
Michael Gettel-Gilmartin:
Middle Grade Fiction   159
Duncan Ellis: Speculative Fiction   167
Crystal Wood: Travel Writing   175
Stephen O'Donnell: Figurative/Narrative Art   183
Sarah Cypher: Literary Fiction,
Manuscript Editing   191

Acknowledgements   199

interviews

Foreword

This collection explores the stories behind the stories. It's a craft book, a how-to guide, a catalogue of successes and failures, and above all, a celebration of creativity and community.

Writing can be a lonely thing to love.

In her interview, Liz Prato talks about the importance of finding one's writing tribe.

When I moved to Portland, Oregon, in 2001, I found mine, thanks to Steve Arndt introducing me to Stevan Allred and Joanna Rose, the Pinewood Table teachers who have encouraged a number of *Brave on the Page* contributors.

Oregon is full of writers who support each other. The forty-two authors in this collection all live in the state or have roots here. They are novelists and journalists. They are essayists and travel writers and poets. They are funny, smart, sad and wise. Some have been traditionally published. Some have been published by small presses or literary journals. Others are unpublished. And yet we all commit the same brave act—confronting the blank page every day. No matter what the cost, no matter what the outcome, we set our other obligations aside to write.

And that's something to celebrate.

A year and a half ago, I launched an interview series on my blog, laurastanfill.wordpress.com, because I love promoting authors and learning what motivates them.

Brave on the Page, the first volume of Forest Avenue Press' Seven Questions Series, grew out of that exploration. I chose to focus on Oregon as a thank you to the rich literary culture that welcomed me when I moved to Portland more than a decade ago. Writing can be lonely, but it doesn't have to be.

The fifteen interviews in this collection were conducted by email between February 2011 and September 2012, then updated (as necessary) and edited for clarity and consistency.

The flash essays at the heart of this book investigate the writer's life from different perspectives. I asked the twenty-seven contributors to pick a question word (such as "who" or "how") and to respond to that prompt in relation to the craft of writing.

So turn the page and find out why, and when, and how, and where, and what we write, and who we are as Oregon writers.

Laura Stanfill
Forest Avenue Press
Portland, Oregon

Interviews

Lauren Kessler:
Narrative Nonfiction

Lauren Kessler actively engages in her material, whether it's working with Alzheimer's patients, sitting through middle school classes or sweating through a two-week fitness bootcamp. She funnels research, interviews and hands-on experience through her own perspective, distilling all that material into award-winning narrative nonfiction. Above all, she's a masterful storyteller with a keen sense of pacing and a journalist's flair for recording pitch-perfect dialogue.

Her new book, *Counterclockwise: One Midlife Woman's Quest to Turn Back the Hands of Time*—a spirited romp through the real science (and the real hucksterism) of the anti-aging movement—is slated for publication in June 2013.

"I write because I'm intensely curious about everything," she said in her 2011 speech at HomeWord Bound, the annual Community Partners for Affordable Housing benefit. "Writing funds that curiosity and gives legitimacy to my nosiness."

When her daughter Lizzie was twelve and thirteen, Lauren focused her investigative zeal on their relationship. She trailed Lizzie to middle school, the mall, summer camp and wrestling practice, while researching teen brains and talking to scores of parents, teachers and other tween and teen experts.

The result, *My Teenage Werewolf: A Mother, A Daughter, A Journey Through the Thicket of Adolescence,* should be required reading for every parent. The book is a brave and honest piece of reporting about the messy necessity of daughters pushing away from their mothers in order to forge their own identities. Lauren tackles some scary subjects—including the alternate selves these "Born Digital" children create online.

Lauren's other books include *Dancing with Rose,* which won the Pacific Northwest Book Award (and is titled *Finding Life in the Land of Alzheimer's* in paperback); *Clever Girl,* a *Washington Post* bestseller; *The Happy Bottom Riding Club,* a *Los Angeles Times* bestseller and *Full Court Press.*

Stubborn Twig, the story of three generations of the Yasui family, was chosen for the Oregon Reads program in 2009 as part of the state's sesquicentennial events. Lauren's interest in subcultures within our midst fuels her work.

"I want—and I need—to learn about these worlds," she said, "and I need readers to see what I see and learn what I learned."

Lauren's work has been published in the *New York Times Magazine*, the *Los Angeles Times Magazine*, *O* (the Oprah magazine), *Ladies' Home Journal*, *Women's Day*, salon.com, newsweek.com and the *Nation*, among others. She is the founder and director of the new multimedia narrative journalism master's program at the University of Oregon's Portland center.

1. Tell us about *Counterclockwise: One Midlife Woman's Quest to Turn Back the Hands of Time*.

My newest book is a frank, funny—and up-close-and-personal—exploration of the hope *and hype* of the anti-aging movement. Bootcamp in Utah in 118-degree heat. A raw foods diet. Hypnosis. Detox. A failed self-compassion test. "Uncomfortable" laser treatments. Watching my face age from twenty to seventy-five via computer magic. Or what about a regimen of bio-identical hormones? What will I subject myself to—and in the process educate my readers about—on my year-long journey to reverse time from the inside out?

Guided by intense curiosity and healthy skepticism, a sense of adventure and a sense of humor, I investigate what it takes to *be* younger, not just look younger. I am at once the careful reporter, the immersion journalist, the self-designated lab rat and a midlife woman who is not interested in being as old as her driver's license insists she is.

My mission isn't about vanity (well, maybe a

little) but about discovering ways to prolong our "health-span," the long midlife years we can spend enjoying high-level energy, robust fitness and physical and creative vitality. I think of this book as part Mary Roach, part A.J. Jacobs—and all me.

2. What's the definition of narrative nonfiction? How is it different from memoir, biography and journalism?

Narrative nonfiction combines the force of fact with the drama of fiction. It meshes authenticity (this really happened, no fabrication) with resonance (this is the crafted, nuanced story of what happened). It is a form that allows a writer both to narrate facts and to search for truth, to blend the empirical eye of the reporter with the moral vision— the I—of the storyteller.

The "narrative" defines how the story is told, the motion and emotion, the creation of narrative arc, character development, scene-setting, action sequences, dialogue and interior monologue. The "nonfiction" defines the assiduously researched factual content.

Genres are often not hard-and-fast categories, but I would say that memoir inhabits the land between nonfiction and fiction, and is most often constructed from memory, not deep research. Biography is usually well researched but often not told in a compelling narrative fashion. And most journalism is about the gathering and logical ordering of facts, not the construction of story.

3. For *My Teenage Werewolf*, you immersed yourself in your daughter's world for eighteen months. Did you study Lizzie the same way you approach other subjects, or did the ultra-personal nature of your research affect your methods? Does all your immersion reporting become personal to some degree?

All writers are immersed in their work, of course, but for me, immersion has a particular and distinct meaning. It is the way I learn about—and learn from—the worlds I want to illuminate for readers. In *Counterclockwise,* it is the fascinating world of anti-aging, from the labs of Nobelists looking for the answer to aging to the Internet hucksters selling the latest magic potion, from raw foodists to detoxers, fitness junkies to Botox queens. I learn about this world not just by reading about it and interviewing the people involved but by involving myself, by becoming that "self-designated lab rat."

In *My Teenage Werewolf,* the world is that of the twenty-first century teen, the cultural, emotional, psychological, even neurological, world teen girls inhabit as well as the intense and tumultuous world of mother-daughter relationships. Immersion, as I practice it, is a cultural anthropologist's tool and mindset... an active, intense observation that continues for so long or is done in such a way that the observer fades into the background. And yes, it was hard (and a continuous challenge) to be both observer and participant in my daughter's life. But it also served to improve our interactions—the distance, the "this will be a great story for the book" comment when we were about to get into a fight—and ultimately our relationship.

I was also an immersion reporter/cultural anthropologist in *Dancing with Rose* (*Finding Life in the Land of Alzheimer's* in paperback) where I took a minimum-wage, in-the-trenches job as a caregiver at an Alzheimer's facility in order to understand the world inhabited by those with this disease.

4. I've been raving about *My Teenage Werewolf*, telling my mom friends to read it before our kids get to middle school. How have mothers of pre-teen and teen girls responded to the book? And how did your daughter Lizzie respond? Did she read the manuscript before it was finished?

First, thanks for raving! The good kind, I mean. I have done a lot of raving in my life—especially when my daughter was between twelve and sixteen (she just turned eighteen)—and it wasn't the good kind…

The response has been just terrific, from emails to comments on the blog where I've continued to write about mother-daughter issues (at myteenage werewolf.com) to Facebook and Twitter chat to actual handwritten letters (gasp). By "terrific," I mean readers are relieved to learn they are not the only ones being driven crazy by their teen (or pre-teen) girl. I mean comforted and amused. It feels good to laugh about this in the midst of what seems like an endless pitched battle. Readers say they've learned a lot from the book (especially about the teen brain) and they thank me for being "Margaret Mead in middle school" so they get a richer understanding of that world. They also talk about the ah-ha moment of realizing what werewolves *they* were when they were teens (I know I was).

I read long passages of the book to my daughter during the writing process—she had veto power over anything—and she read most of the manuscript before it became a book.

This book would not have been possible without her. She had to buy into it completely, so she felt from the beginning that she held the power. She was my guide to the teen girl world. She was my insider source. She was my expert. So the experience actually empowered her, I think. Her reaction was very positive. She appeared with me (reading her lines of dialogue) at several bookstore and library events. That was *her* idea, not mine!

Now, of course, the book is old, old news. She doesn't give it a thought.

5. Tell us a little about your writing process. Do you write and research at the same time, or do you complete your research first? Please describe a typical writing day.

It's never a clean division. I need to know the shape and direction of the story before I start to write, so I do a significant amount of research just to discover the narrative line, to feel the movement in the story, to know who the characters are. But I am also often in the midst of immersion while I write. I find that it keeps the narrative fresh and exciting.

So, with *Counterclockwise*, I declared April to be "detox month." I both, shall we say, "cleansed" and wrote about it simultaneously. Not a great month. Same thing with exploring superfoods and raw foods, and with many other things I did for the book. I would go in for a muscle biopsy in the morning and write about it in the afternoon. But, while writing, I'd be amplifying, filling in the blanks, enriching the narrative with research I had already completed.

My days can be quite different depending on whether I am in the midst of an immersion experience or just sitting in front of my computer. I always exercise before I write—go for a run, work out at the gym, etc. It gives me the energy I need, boosts my mood and gives me brainless time that is often the richest time to process the work. I write about five hours a day. I really, really try to not write any longer. I sit on a big red stability ball. I drink probably eight cups of tea (some green but mostly herbal) while writing. Sometimes I chain-chew Orbit Sweet Mint gum. I think that's enough detail.

6. You are the director of the multimedia journalism master's program at the University of Oregon. What does "multimedia" entail? Has technology changed the fundamentals of reporting?

The program is all about adding tools to the storyteller's toolbox, enhancing the nonfiction storytelling process by expanding the ways a tale can be told. So you're a writer who uses words to tell stories. Great. But sometimes sound is the richest way to tell a story, and sometimes still images are the most powerful, and sometimes it's video.

The program is all about The Story—how to think story, and how to report for story (which may involve one person with a pen and a pad of paper or a team with lights and mics and cameras). It's about figuring out the very best, most compelling, most audience-accessible way to tell stories. And doing it.

And yes, technology has an impact. But technology changes from minute to minute. There's a new gadget announced every week, a new app, a new device. It's impossible to keep up. The fundamentals of nonfiction storytelling stand outside and *above* technology, and they do *not* change: the art of conceptualizing a story, of finding the motion and emotion of the story, the imperative to be honest and thorough and accurate and compassionate about a story, the responsibility to maintain the highest of ethics. That's what this is all about.

7. What advice do you have for aspiring nonfiction authors?

I wrote a piece, now much anthologized, a while ago called "The Ten Stupid Things Writers Do to Mess Up Their Lives." It's all about self-sabotage. Writers are masterful at this. It contains my best advice—and what I tell myself on a regular basis.

Here's the link: laurenkessler.com/essays/the-ten-stupid-things-writers-do-to-mess-up-their-lives.

Lauren's website is laurenkessler.com. Her Counterclockwise *blog is counterclockwisebook.com. Lauren and her daughter Lizzie blog together at myteenagewerewolf.com.*

Yuvi Zalkow:
Literary Fiction, 'Failure Conduit'

Yuvi Zalkow draws people into his story worlds with witty lines and well-chosen details about the missteps of winsomely obsessive characters. His smart, sincere brand of humor conveys heart and heartbreak. And he challenges storytelling conventions with apparent ease—and without losing the reader.

Yuvi's debut novel, *A Brilliant Novel in the Works*, was released in August 2012 by MP Publishing. It is an incisive portrait of the act of creation and its effect on relationships. At the beginning, the protagonist, a writer named Yuvi, stands on his desk in his underwear with a blank piece of paper underfoot, afraid to engage in the act of writing.

In this mind-boggling, crazy quilt of a novel, Yuvi stitches present-tense scenes together with short, elegant stories ostensibly written by the neurotic but lovable protagonist Yuvi (but of course really written by the author). The blurring of the line between fiction and memoir gives this playful book a powerful emotional punch. Amid riffs on Protestant sandwiches and pantslessness, there are honest moments of connection and disconnection.

Yuvi is the creator of the "I'm a Failed Writer" video series, which he publishes online at Writer Unboxed and on his website, yuvizalkow.com. His work has appeared in the *LA Review, Narrative Magazine, Rosebud, Carve Magazine* and the *Clackamas Literary Review,* among others. His story "God and Buses" was published in *Glimmer Train,* Spring 2011, Issue 78.

Yuvi, a Portland, Oregon, resident, earned a master's degree in creative writing from Antioch University, and he's a technical writer by trade.

1. Tell us about *A Brilliant Novel in the Works*. What does it feel like to have your book out in the world? I think it would be especially interesting to ask Yuvi, your protagonist, how he feels.

On the surface, it's a novel about a neurotic Jew writing a novel, but it stretches beyond that conceit, confronting issues about how a man deals with the crooked aspects of marriage and family.

The novel started by mistake, which I'm sure isn't so uncommon for writers. I was simultaneously writing a lot of personal essays about my childhood in Georgia while writing a story about this neurotic writer who was struggling with his writing (and with his gentile wife) (and with his sexual perversions) (and with his brother-in-law's gastrointestinal troubles), and then I realized that these two projects were colliding. The essays informed the fiction and the fiction informed the essays. I actually lost track of what were real stories and what were made-up stories.

The experience of publishing and promoting this book has been a crazy ride for me, thrilling and horrifying at the same time. On one hand, I've been dreaming about publishing this book for years. But also, my list of worries has only grown because of this enhanced exposure.

As for the Yuvi character in my novel… Well, I'm sure it's pretty clear to most readers that I toy with the boundary between fiction and memoir. And this character's list of worries isn't so different from my own. But I really don't know how he would function in this phase of his own novel's development. As I started envisioning the end of my book, it was more about an emotional and relational sort of growth for my protagonist than about him getting his novel published. Maybe we'll deal with that issue in the sequel. (Just kidding. Though friends tease me that I should write *Another Brilliant Novel in the Works*.)

2. What are you working on now?

I'm writing a more regular novel. By regular, I mean I still couldn't get away from Georgia (and Jews), but this time it's about Polish Jewish immigrants who move to rural Georgia in 1938. Finally, a story that doesn't have Yuvi in it as the main character. It's pretty challenging trying to keep this thing on the tracks, but it's been a great exploration for me. I think (I hope) (*ppppplease* let it be true!!!) that I'm learning how to write something more than just an autobiographical story. This one is taking me deeper into other people's minds and it's going well, though I wish it were moving faster.

3. Your writing is laugh-out-loud funny without sacrificing content, characterization or weight. Any tips on being hilarious on the page?

Wow. Thank you for the kind words.

Hmmm. Tips. Well, for me it starts with shame. I'm oozing with shame. But it's more than just shame. Shame alone is pretty tedious to read about. Once I went through enough therapists to stop taking myself so seriously, then my shame started to come off funny. I actually had not even thought of this stuff as funny until I started reading my work to others (thank you Stevan Allred and Joanna Rose!). Who would've thought it was funny that I pee sitting down because I'm too nervous to do it standing?

4. The Failed Writer video series is entertaining, original and helpful for other writers. How did the series start? What happens to the Failed Writer concept now that you've succeeded as a novelist?

The video stuff started because I had to give a lecture in order to graduate from Antioch with an MFA. I was terrified of giving the lecture but I knew I had a lot to say about the persistence required for the submission process. So I pre-recorded a twenty-minute presentation to get the audience warmed up without requiring me to perform on the spot. Anyway, the lecture went just fine (both the pre-recorded part and the live part), but more interesting was that making the video was a blast. So I kept on experimenting, taking the videos further and further each time so that they now cover all kinds of writerly topics and are full of bad stick figure drawings and stop-motion animation of my toddler's stuffed animals.

People have been asking me about whether I can keep calling myself a failed writer now that I have a published book. But I think it is just as relevant as ever to consider myself a failed writer. Probably more important now. Even though I'm very excited about the book, there are plenty of potential failures ahead that I can look forward to: bad reviews, failed subsequent novels and so on.

But I think even more important than my future failures is that this whole Failed Writer shtick came about from my state of mind, which didn't have so much to do with the specific successes or failures along the way.

If you follow my videos (especially Failed Writer Episode #7: "Failing as a Failed Failure"), you know that this attitude has both positive qualities and negative qualities. On the downside, I probably feel more shame and self-loathing than what is healthy; on the upside, I'm constantly trying to learn how to do things better. I'll always be a failure, some days more successfully than others.

5. Wow, Yuvi, you write fiction, you have a family, you're a tech writer—and you even earned a master's degree in creative writing from Antioch University while juggling those major commitments. How do you fit everything into your life? Scheduling? Prioritizing? (Do you sleep?)

I'm a pretty obsessive to-do list maker. Sheri (my wife) will tell you the absurd degree to which I rely on my task management software (mmm… OmniFocus). I don't do anything that OmniFocus hasn't approved of. If OmniFocus told me to jump off a bridge, I'd do it—especially if it told me which bridge to use and which project this task was associated with. But it's not honestly as bad as it sounds. These lists of tasks still leave room for me to discover new, interesting things along the way. For instance, one item on the list might be just to write something new for a half hour. I use these lists to get a rough feeling for the most valuable ways I might use the limited time I have available so I don't end up squandering it too badly.

Also, having a baby was awfully effective in teaching me to focus on the most essential things. It's amazing how many things you can drop on the floor without getting arrested. But I try not to drop the big things: the family, the writing, the martinis.

6. Your persistence to find homes for your stories has earned many acceptances from literary journals—and many rejections, too. Tell us about

your quest to get a story published in *Glimmer Train.* **Any advice for writers who are frustrated by rejections?**

A *Glimmer Train* publication was something I'd been dreaming of for more than ten years. My "Poop to Glimmer" video talks about this in more detail but I just found a way to work the submission process into my life without ever taking it too seriously, or too lightly. I don't know if this works for all writers, but I just tried to keep submitting at a certain rate (say ten places a month with various stories) without even thinking about it too much. I'd get a rejection and I'd mark that submission off the list and that simply meant I had another one to send out. I was more like a detached secretary with regard to this process. Sounds kind of boring, huh? Unfortunately, one of the tasks I've dropped on the floor recently is my submission regimen. But I'm allowing myself to mostly focus on the novel writing for now.

7. In "From Poop to Glimmer," you mention rereading as a way to analyze and understand great stories, such as Tobias Wolff's "The Liar." Please share some more of your favorites. Why have these particular works amazed or inspired you?

I've always been drawn to a strong voice. The storyteller has to grab me quick. I honestly think I'm too slow and dumb a reader to stick with a difficult or awkward storyteller. I know I've missed out on some great literature because of this weakness, but that's the way I am.

As for short stories, I've studied Raymond Carver and Tobias Wolff quite closely. They're great storytellers. Also there's this short story ("Conversion of the Jews") from one of Philip Roth's first books that I keep returning to as I re-think the concept of a character arc. And Tim O'Brien's "The Things They Carried" (I'm talking about the short story in this case) is relentless and amazing and worth studying closely for how that story builds and builds.

As for some of the novels I've been obsessed with, there's *The Razor's Edge* by Somerset Maugham. I'm amazed how effectively the narrator gets away with how he tells that story. *Billy Bathgate* by E.L. Doctorow has an amazing authority to the voice. *Herzog* by Saul Bellow is shocking to me in how Bellow tells a story in third person that seems closer in to the man's consciousness than even a first person account could render.

Oh. Also. James Baldwin's story "Sonny's Blues" blew my pants off it was so good.

Is that a good way to end this discussion? With pantslessness? And even if my pants hyperbole doesn't work, you should read "Sonny's Blues."

Stop by yuvizalkow.com to learn more about Yuvi and to watch his Failed Writer videos.

Kim Cooper Findling:
Memoir

Chance of Sun reads like an honest love letter to the state of Oregon.

Kim Cooper Findling's memoir is a beautiful map of her own journey, starting with a Rogue River backpacking trip in 1975, when she was five. But it's also a stirring depiction of what it's like to be an Oregonian.

In *Chance of Sun*, Kim recounts her adventures growing up in North Bend and the choices she made along the path to adulthood. The short, linked essays are surprising, resonant and deeply moving.

Many people who call Oregon home are from elsewhere, which makes Kim's book even more important to the cultural landscape. It was published in 2011 by Nestucca Spit Press, run by prolific author and editor Matt Love.

"Kim is an entirely fresh (and welcome) voice for Oregon, and her memoir of growing up in Oregon in the '70s and '80s is completely novel in its perspective," Matt said.

A chapter of *Chance of Sun* won the 2011 *Oregon Quarterly* Northwest Perspectives Essay Contest. The book is available directly through Nestucca Spit Press, at several indie bookstores in Oregon and through Amazon as an e-book.

Kim is the editor of *Central Oregon Magazine* and the Central Oregon ambassador for Travel Oregon's Ask Oregon program. She writes and edits for magazines and professional organizations, and she teaches writing workshops.

1. Tell us about your memoir, *Chance of Sun*.

Chance of Sun is a coming of age story set in Oregon. The story is a meditation on nature, love and search for self, with a significant dark twist. Much of the narrative takes place in the small towns and woods of Oregon, and includes such '70s and '80s Oregon antics as looking for a boyfriend in a campground, visiting the Shakespeare Fest in Ashland and fishing for rockfish off the coast. But the story's climax is in Portland, where I became caught up in the wild life for a while in my twenties. It didn't go well (she says dryly). That disaster shapes the rest of the (my) story.

Matt Love says my book is about finding myself, losing myself and finding myself again, all in relationship to my connection to Oregon.

2. How did writing about your life change your view of what it means to be an Oregonian?

Any epiphanies about the state or its impact on your identity?

Oh, wow. I didn't think I could fall deeper in love with Oregon, and yet this book made me do so. I've lived in Oregon my whole life, aside from a few months-long stints here and there, and I think it had been difficult for me to get outside of the state, so to speak, in my head.

I had underestimated, or perhaps just hadn't properly considered, the value of my small-town Oregon childhood. (As I've joked, I never thought my fabulous Coos County upbringing would get me a book deal.)

What has been most wonderful about this process is the opportunity to chronicle the details of growing up in rural Oregon in the '70s and '80s and then connect with people who shared these same experiences. Here we were, all along, kind of under the radar, thinking our stories didn't amount to much.

Through this book as a vehicle, I've met so many small-town kids and realized how real and cool and funny and awesome they are. We have much to celebrate, not discount, about our simple, quirky upbringings. It's an amazing thing to have people approach me and say, "You wrote my story" or "Your book feels like home." My sister describes it as "finding your people." And it's finding my people all over again that made me fall in love with Oregon even more.

3. Matt Love is an important chronicler of Oregon history. What was it like working with Nestucca Spit Press and adding your personal story to Matt's impressive collection of nonfiction about the state?

It was amazing and fantastic. I met Matt at a reading at a bookstore in Bend during the summer of 2009 and it was utter serendipity. Matt is such a champion of Oregon and its people and their adventures. He is also a great teacher who is passionate about authentic stories told well with really great writing. He immediately became my advocate and challenger. Working with him was invigorating, personal, motivating, empowering and daunting— he demands excellence. I loved every minute of it. Well, when I wasn't sobbing over the keyboard.

Simultaneous to writing *Chance of Sun* and working with Matt, I was writing a travel book for a big press back east. The contrast was really interesting. Distributing a book through a small press has its challenges, but it's also much more personal and rich with experience. I am glad to have had both experiences, but especially proud and grateful that my own story, in *Chance of Sun*, was handled by a small Oregon press, and by Matt.

4. You've also written a travel book, *Day Trips from Portland, Oregon: Getaway Ideas for the Local Traveler*, which was published by Globe Pequot Press in 2011. Is travel writing as fun as it seems? What was the hardest part?

I've been a travel writing for more than a decade and sometimes marvel at how I got so lucky. Becoming an "Oregon travel expert" feels like a happy accident to me. I've lived in the state my whole life, and in so many places in Oregon. In each I always exercised my innate wanderlust. This led me naturally to write about traveling Oregon. I did that enough times, and voila—expert. Great example of that old saying about "do what you love and the opportunity will follow."

Travel writing is so much fun. It is also work. I've passed many a vacation with my head stuck in a notebook (or these days, taking notes and photos with my iPhone).

Just yesterday, on a bike ride at Black Butte Ranch, my five-year-old said, "Mom, leave your phone be!" But someday she'll understand that the reason we, as a family, enjoy so many Oregon adventures is because of Mom's job. There is nothing I love more than hitting the road to see more of this state. Even when I think I'm tired, my wanderlust kicks in within a week or two.

The hardest part of *Day Trips* was completing the project by deadline, which was a mere nine weeks after I signed the contract. Very empowering to learn that I can actually write 70,000 edited words in sixty-three days, as well as keep the children alive and not lose my mind (much). During those same nine weeks, my oldest started kindergarten, I turned forty, and my mother was diagnosed with cancer. It was complete insanity. And yet in the end everything worked out. I like being reminded of that from time to time.

5. What was one of the most unusual or memorable places you visited as part of your *Day Trips* research?

Given that nine-week time crunch, you won't be surprised to learn that I didn't go anywhere while I was writing *Day Trips* except to my home office, wearing my pajamas. Luckily I'd been traveling Oregon for forty years and writing about it for ten and had plenty to draw upon. But the process did serve to remind me of so many awesome Oregon places. I took the kids to the Enchanted Forest last summer, hit the Oregon Country Fair for the first time since college, toured the historic Columbia River Highway and will revisit Astoria soon. Many more places remain on my list, including the old drive-in movie theater on Highway 99, the Oregon Vortex, wine country and Wildlife Safari. What an amazing state we live in!

6. Kim, you write and edit professionally for various magazines and organizations. How did you get started in the business? Do you have advice for aspiring freelance writers?

Sometimes even I forget how much rejection and persistence this route required. But I wanted it. That's my advice—if you really want it, keep at it. I quit my job in 2000 and went to a writers' conference to learn the basics of magazine writing. Then I dove in to querying, pitching and submitting. Eventually, it worked. I broke in with a few essay pieces and began to get assignments. After that it was just a matter of more persistence. I'm teaching writing here and there now, which feels like such a wonderful full-circle to my experience.

More advice: read, write, listen and observe as much as humanly possible.

7. You're currently working on a novel and a memoir. What are they about, and how do you balance working on two big projects?

The novel is about an Oregon girl who runs away from summer camp. The memoir is, loosely, about love, death, motherhood and laughing until you pee your pants. Having two very different projects enables me to manipulate my innate, Libra-born inability to settle on anything for very long. When I'm working on nonfiction, I want to write fiction and vice versa. In this way, hopefully, I lurch forward toward a completed project.

Learn more about Kim at kimcooperfindling.com. Find Chance of Sun *at your local bookstore, or visit Nestucca Spit Press, nestuccaspitpress.com, to order it.*

Liz Prato:
Stories, Novels, Classes

Through her involvement with various organizations, Liz—a short story writer, novelist, essayist and writing teacher—has established herself as a fixture on the local writing scene.

She has been featured as a panelist and teacher at Wordstock, Portland's annual literary festival, and as a guest speaker at Willamette Writers. She teaches writing classes at The Attic and Annie Bloom's Bookstore. And she runs Write in Portland, writepdx.blogspot.com, an online calendar of local literary classes and events.

While her characters struggle to fix their lives and to reinterpret their own sense of themselves, Liz's well-developed authorial voice is strikingly honest. Her language is tightly focused but also infused with brushstrokes of poetry and refreshing doses of humor and candor. Her novel, *The Lost Art of Miracles*, explores some of the same themes as her shorter work—identity, sexuality and grief.

Liz's work has been widely published in magazines as well as the Soft Skull Press anthology *Who's Your Mama,* and she has earned four prestigious Pushcart nominations. She was recently awarded a Tennessee Williams Scholarship to the Sewanee Writers' Conference. Check out her most recently published piece, "This Is Your Birth Certificate," in the 25th anniversary issue of *Hayden's Ferry Review.*

1. You're a rare breed of writer, one who switches successfully between short stories, novels and even nonfiction. How has working on short pieces influenced your longer work, or vice versa? What are you focused on now?

I started writing short stories because I thought it would make me a better novelist. And, in some ways, it did, by helping me be more concise, by figuring how to "get to it."

You don't have a lot of time to make an impact in a short story or essay, and there's no reason that rule shouldn't apply to a novel as well. At the same time, the space of a novel helps my shorter pieces by teaching me how to fully explore character.

Right now I'm focusing on the short form— stories and essays. Love them. Love.

2. Please tell us about your novel, *The Lost Art of Miracles.*

It's the story of a twenty-something guy named Cam who moves to Santa Fe a few months after his brother kills himself. He's hoping to just hide away from his friends and family—and himself—everyone who wants him to "move on" or "heal" or be normal again. Like that's possible after losing someone you love. He becomes friends with a gay artist named Bill, whose lover died the previous year. Instead of being able to hide from himself, Cam ends up having to face questions of sexual orientation that he's been trying to push down for years, largely because his brother was homophobic. In trying to come to terms with his identity, Cam has to confront his grief. Sounds like a barrel of laughs, right? The good news is that with a bunch of gay men on the page, there's a lot of humor. It's not all sturm und drang. That's just not my style—in real life, and on the page. Humor is not an accessory. It's a life preserver.

I'm also working on a new novel about a gay man raising his teenage son with his partner, eight years after his wife abandoned them. When the novel begins, the mother returns to their lives, creating chaos. But it turns out she endured a trauma many years earlier, which she kept secret (based on the real-life events of the Pan-Am bombing over Lockerbie, Scotland, in 1988), and we see how deep the ripples of a tragedy can extend.

3. Over the past few years, you have studied—and mastered—the nuances of point of view. What led you to that trajectory? What's the biggest thing you've learned from your explorations?

Oh, wow. That's really nice of you to say, although I wouldn't say I've "mastered" it. I'm constantly studying, trying to figure it out, and every time I think I have a good grasp on point of view, I read something that totally turns me upside down again. I ended up exploring point of view mainly because I was—unsuccessfully—always trying to tell too many characters' stories through a singular POV. So I started experimenting with POV to see how it could open up my worlds.

What I've learned is that strong narrative stance is almost invisible, so readers and beginning writers don't know how it's operating. They don't know it even exists. I think a real understanding of narrative stance is the main thing that separates decent writers from really good writers.

4. You're very active in the Portland writing community. In fact, it seems you know just about everybody. Why did you decide to engage with other local writers, and how has that involvement changed your perspective on the profession?

Well, I've been lucky. Writers are pretty generous folks, and a lot of people—in and out of Portland—offered their support to me from early on. Steve Almond, Cheryl Strayed, David Leavitt, to name a few. Those relationships have been an essential piece of my career successes. And becoming a teacher automatically immersed me in a certain level of community, too.

But, more than anything, I think community is necessary to a bunch of people who spend all day thinking about characters who, in the minds of other people, don't even exist. I mean, come on. It's not just when we're in front of our computers. We're doing it when we're showering or cooking dinner, too. God, we might even be doing it while we're making love. And what's even weirder is, unlike other people we love, we're not trying to make our characters' lives easier. We're thinking of ways to thoroughly fuck them up. When you're doing something that crazy—and undervalued, in a culture obsessed with poorly behaved celebrities—you need a tribe. We keep each other sane, and we give each other a hand whenever we can.

5. Tell me about your teaching career. What kinds of classes do you offer? What have you learned about the craft from working with your students?

Like my writing, my classes are diverse. I teach creative nonfiction and fiction workshops, at the Attic Institute, and privately at Annie Bloom's Books. We not only critique the participants' pieces in progress, but also study craft essays and analyze published work. That was missing from the workshop method through which I learned to write, so I like to round out my classes with a good heaping of both.

I also teach these really fun two-hour seminars on a specific topic, like point of view or how to submit to literary journals. I love teaching short stories, but everyone wants to write a novel or memoir these days. It seems crazy to me. It takes years to write and revise a book, and then there's a ninety-eight percent chance it won't get published. In short stories and essays you get to explore different themes and voices and characters, and the time investment isn't such a killer. A while back I read a *New York Times* article about why so many writers abandon novels, and Michael Chabon said something like, he had to abandon an early novel because it was trying to kill him.

What I've learned most about craft from my students is probably what I said earlier about narrative stance—that when it's done well, it's invisible. It's kind of like watching Jimmy Stewart act. It's so effortless, you don't realize he's acting.

6. It seems like you reached a point in your writing life where you committed to being a professional in the industry. You set goals and started meeting them with discipline, determination and skill. What advice would you give to writers who are just beginning to take their own careers seriously?

Oh, man. Quit bitching and just do it. Plenty of writers—talented writers—spend a lot of time complaining to me about how they don't have the time, or the energy, to focus on their writing enough to really gain some momentum. And, sure, we all struggle with that. But the writers who are truly serious about it as a career make time. They make sacrifices.

There was one time I was asked to join a kick-ass writers' group, and I almost turned it down because

I didn't want to give up a night of my free time. Thank god my husband, and my good friend Yuvi Zalkow, gently reminded me of how often I despair over how I'll become better at my craft. Did I think it was just going to be handed to me? No. I was going to have to work for it. I was going to have to give up something. And what did I really give up? Watching "What Not to Wear" in real time.

So my advice to new writers is: be honest with yourself. And be gentle with yourself, too. Be honest about how badly you want a writing career, and what you're willing to give up for it. Then accept whatever your absolute truth is. If the most you're willing to give up is an hour a week, then make peace with knowing that right now your career can't develop at a lightning pace. This is the most you can do right now, and that's okay. And know whatever you decide isn't carved in stone. The circumstances of our lives can change with alarming speed, so you can change your priorities, too.

7. You're a thoughtful reader of other people's work. What novels or stories have impressed you in the past year or two? Why?

Oh, thanks for saying that. It's really kind—and important to me. Mary Robison's *Why Did I Ever?* knocked my socks off. It's been out for several years, but I just finally got to it. She's got an insane economy of words, without sacrificing character or story. And she's brave enough to write unlikeable female characters who we somehow end up rooting for. A memoir in a similar style that inspired me immensely is Bill Clegg's *Portrait of An Addict As a Young Man.* It's brutally honest and beautifully written. I tore through it, then instantly wanted to read it again.

I'm also a big fan of a great story called "Housewiverly Arts" by Megan Mayhew Bergman. It's quirky, but not self-consciously so. It has a strong sense of authority, the kind that lets readers know they're in good hands. There are plenty of mature, well-published authors who don't have that kind of easy authority. That's what a reader really wants, consciously or not. They want to trust that whatever crazy-ass ride the writer takes them on will be handled with grace.

For more information about Liz Prato, check out her website, lizprato.com.

Shasta Kearns Moore:
Children's Literature

Some people seem like they do it all. Shasta Kearns Moore is one of them. She's a journalist, a blogger and the mom of identical twins, as well as the author of a new children's book, *Dark & Light: A Love Story in Black and White,* and a novella, *A Twist of Fate.*

Dark & Light, a sturdy board book, features baby-friendly black-and-white images and an uplifting story about identity and sharing.

Shasta used Kickstarter, the online fundraising site, to accrue more than $10,000—twice as much as her original goal—toward publishing *Dark & Light.* The proceeds will help pay for her son Malachi's cerebral palsy treatments.

JJ and Malachi were born ten weeks premature in June 2010, and a brain bleed caused Malachi's cerebral palsy. Shasta began chronicling her experience with her boys on her blog, OutrageousFortune.net, in February 2011. She employs the same sparkling, concise style she developed in the newspaper world, but now she's applying her facility with language to the challenges she's facing in her own life.

Shasta has that rare gift of being able to describe exactly what she's going through, no matter how heartbreaking or frustrating. Her blog is as much about hope for the future as it is about her day-to-day obstacles and the research she's been doing about cerebral palsy in the hopes of helping her son.

1. Tell us about *Dark & Light: A Love Story in Black and White* and your plan for a trilogy.

Dark & Light is a really fun book that is unlike anything I've seen in the young children's market. It's an elegantly simple board book that uses the universal concepts of black and white to tell a story about the origin of stars, the moon, lightning and even the shades of gray. The second and third books continue to blend the simplicity of black, white, grays and colors with natural elements—rainbows, hurricanes and the ocean—to create stories that entertain young and old alike. The first book was released in October 2012 with the other two following sometime in 2013.

2. What gave you the idea to write and publish a children's book, and how will you use the proceeds? How did Kickstarter help you jumpstart this project?

The idea came after realizing that my twin boys thoroughly enjoyed books with very simple images —not watercolors or pencil drawings, as in many children's books, but silhouettes in bold contrast. The trouble was these sorts of books had almost no plot and were very boring for me to "read" over and over again. I thought there must be a way for a book with simple images to also have an interesting story, so I set about creating one.

The treatment we use for Malachi's cerebral palsy ended up being a very integral part of this book becoming a reality. The Anat Baniel Method talks a lot about how the brain learns through simple concepts that build on each other until they create a more complex web of knowledge. I think that's why babies and children with functional needs enjoy *Dark & Light* so much—because it talks about real, concrete things in a way they can see and understand.

But Malachi's lessons in the Anat Baniel Method are very expensive and we needed to find a way to continue to afford them. I got the idea to use Kickstarter—a crowd-source funding website for creative projects—to fund start-up costs to print and promote *Dark & Light*.

The results were overwhelming. We ended up raising more than twice our $5,000 goal and had numerous media outlets run stories on us, including the *Huffington Post*. I am so grateful to all of the 260 donors as well as the approximately 800 people who shared and retweeted our cause to their friends. It was truly inspiring.

All of the profits from the book will go directly to Malachi's medical needs, minus ten percent, which will be "paid forward" to other kids with functional needs. In this way, I am marrying the two greatest goals in my life: to become a published author and to do everything I can to maximize Malachi's potential.

3. What's your novella about, Shasta?

Oh good, I've been working on my elevator pitch for *A Twist of Fate*. Here goes:

Three women—a coke-addicted New York City stripper, an Orange County gold trader's business-savvy daughter and a water-fetching slumdog in Mumbai—suddenly switch lives. They discover the personality traits that got them into trouble in their own lives lead to success and happiness in their counterparts' lives. But when they are rotated again into the second woman's life, those same traits lead very quickly to certain death.

So, that's the story. But what it's about is that people are often blamed for the bad situations they are in because there must be something wrong with them, but I wanted to show how those same traits can be good in the right circumstances.

4. You wrote your novella while your boys were babies, and now, with two-year-olds on your hands, you're publishing a children's book. How do you find time to write? Is there any advice you want to share with other new moms?

Sure, marry an awesome husband like mine. He has always made it a priority to give me time to write, either by taking the boys away himself or agreeing to use some of the money he makes to hire a nanny once a week. I couldn't do it if I didn't have such a supportive partner.

That said, though, I think there's a drive in me to always do more and go further. Even now I find myself fretting that I haven't written any fiction in a while and my blog is starting to slip—because I'm doing all the things to start a publishing company all while tending to intensive ABM sessions that we can now afford for Malachi and maintaining a household with another two-year-old. It even sounds crazy to me when I say it out loud.

And I don't really think it's an attribute a person should try to emulate, either. But I do get a measure of satisfaction and self-worth from working on my own projects and everybody should have something in their lives that gives them energy instead of draining it away.

5. As a journalist you learned how to churn out massive amounts of copy on deadline. There's no time for writer's block. Did you find yourself stuck at any point while working on *A Twist of Fate*, or were you able to approach your story like an assignment and just keep going?

Oh yeah, I was stuck a lot. I got the idea for this book... I dunno... years ago. When my world collapsed due to risk factors with my pregnancy and I had to go on bed rest for ten weeks, that would have been a perfect time to write, right? I think I only wrote two scenes that whole time. I just couldn't get motivated.

One thing that really worked was buying a software program called Scrivener (any kickbacks, Scrivener?), which helped me organize my story and break it down into doable chunks. So then it wasn't like: "I HAVE TO WRITE A WHOLE NOVEL." It was like: "Oh yeah, what should I write about for this scene?"

6. Your blog, OutrageousFortune.net, focuses on your personal journey of raising identical twin boys, JJ and Malachi. When and why did you start chronicling your experiences and Malachi's cerebral palsy diagnosis? How has the process of writing about your family enhanced or expanded your life as a new mom?

I started in February 2011 after a local mom of a boy with cerebral palsy got me in touch with the author of LoveThatMax.com. After reading that blog, I posted "To blog or not to blog" on Facebook and a surprising number of people urged me to blog. I had avoided writing for almost a year because I felt like if I was going to spend my precious free time on anything it should be freelance work, but I didn't have the energy for that.

It feels really good to write the blog, though, and I'm glad I can talk about what's going on in my life in a way that can help others (known and unknown) understand a little more about what it's like to have a son with a brain injury. Having a special needs kid is very isolating because it's so rare and nobody knows quite how to talk to you about it. I hope my blog helps people feel a little more comfortable about people with disabilities.

But mostly, I'm just writing for me. It's been wonderful to write again after going so long without that outlet.

7. Your blog posts are so beautifully written, honest and sometimes heartbreaking, and in a short time, you've earned a lot of devoted followers. What feedback have you received from the blogosphere? And how have you gotten your name out there?

Oh, thank you. The feedback from the blogosphere has been ninety-nine percent positive, which I'm frankly surprised at. I've only gotten one mean, nasty comment and I've written some pretty controversial stuff and allow anonymous comments. Dare I hope that the Internet is maturing a little?

Hmmm... probably not.

Well, maybe even the mean nasties have a soft spot for grieving moms.

As for how I've gotten my name out there, I think the vast majority of the traffic started from my very supportive Facebook friends (and their Facebook friends and so on). I follow and comment on several blogs and I've joined a few blog networking groups.

I also think that the disability community is pretty tightly knit. I mean, you have to go through some rough shit to be part of it, so there's a sense of instant camaraderie. People with whom I might otherwise have very little in common are now friends and help me out.

Check out DarkandLightBooks.com for more information. Shasta's blog is OutrageousFortune.net.

Kristy Athens:
Cross-Genre Nonfiction

Opening Kristy Athens' new book is like settling in for an intimate fireside chat with an old friend. In *Get Your Pitchfork On!: The Real Dirt on Country Living*, she tells you everything she knows about rural life while peppering the facts with humorous asides and plenty of anecdotes.

Get Your Pitchfork On! was released in April 2012 as the seventh volume of Process Media's Self-Reliance Series. The 341-page book is a modern and enjoyably personal take on the venerable how-to guide. It's packed with information on everything from chimney maintenance to the truth about mountain lions.

Kristy and her husband Mike spent six years living in the Columbia Gorge. What they learned forms the backbone of the book. Kristy isn't afraid of explaining what went wrong in their experiment with country living; in fact, many chapters offer hilarious and informative first-hand accounts of how *not* to do something. It's these insights that make *Get Your Pitchfork On!* an interesting read even for those who aren't yearning for land of their own. And if you are dreaming of a country home, read this book before you commit.

Kristy has published short fiction and creative nonfiction in various magazines, newspapers and journals, including *Culinate, High Desert Journal, Northwest Palate* and *Portland Monthly.*

1. Tell us about your new book, *Get Your Pitchfork On!: The Real Dirt on Country Living.*

Get Your Pitchfork On! is a primer for urban people who dream of moving to the country. My husband Mike and I owned seven acres on the Washington side of the Columbia River Gorge. We had four buildings, eight to ten chickens, a dog and then a cat.

The book has five sections: Land; Buildings, Inside and Out; Animals; Food; and Community, Family and Culture. The book is sort of between genres—I call it a "how-to with stories."

2. Kristy, when and why did you decide to write about your experience in the Columbia River Gorge? Did putting your anecdotes on the page cause any new revelations about your six years in the country?

I started to think about writing a book after we moved to our land in 2003. I had been reading about "the country" for a few years, and had started learning to garden in Portland. I found that the existing books were great but that most of them were written in the 1970s. Some of the information was hopelessly outdated, and there was no mention of things like cell phone coverage, which turned out to be a big problem at our house. So, I thought maybe an update was in order.

The first piece I wrote was an essay about how much harder everything was to do than Mike and I had imagined. I sold it to *Portland Monthly* magazine, and they ran it in 2006. I wrote an essay about dressing a quail in *Northwest Palate* in 2008.

I was still mostly interested in fiction at the time, and I had two great jobs, one as community relations coordinator for the hospice and one as editor of a local lifestyle magazine. Very busy with those jobs, I was making notes for a book but not really progressing much with it.

Meanwhile, I started to get involved in local politics. This is in the book—I did not understand the ways of the small town, and played with fire and got burned. I lost both jobs, separate incidents, within a month of each other at the end of 2006.

This was, as you can imagine, quite a blow. But what's important is I finally identified what was really missing from all those romance-of-country-living books—how to live in a rural community as a newcomer. When my husband and I had to sell our house, I was devastated but realized that I would be able to talk about my experiences with a truthfulness that I would never dare to employ if I were still living there.

3. Your book covers many facets of rural life. How did you organize such a wealth of material? Did you use an outline?

The manuscript was a real mess for a while! All of my prose is short—usually 1,000 to 1,500 words. So, for my own sanity, I couldn't think of the book as a book—I had to think of it as a series of short pieces.

At first, I just wrote what interested me at the time. I skipped around; I didn't worry about transitions or flow; I just cranked out the content. After a while, I started to think about how to organize it. Most of it was pretty clear-cut, but then you'd have something like deer—are they pests? Beautiful wild creatures? Dinner? Where should they go in the book? That was a little trickier.

4. The food section of *Get Your Pitchfork On!* offers useful information about gardening, composting, canning, dehydrating and "wildcrafting." Now that you're back in the city, do you have a garden or do you frequent farmers' markets? Does your rural background affect your food choices in the city?

We were eating organic food long before we moved to Washington, so having lived on land is not such an influence; more a confirmation of ideals. But I did learn to can while I was in the country, and I made blueberry jam last summer. That felt good.

We are currently renting a house in Southeast Portland and I've been too busy with a full-time job, artwork and *Get Your Pitchfork On!* to focus on gardening much. A couple friends have had me over to their houses this spring to ask me questions about their gardens, which has been fun. I am definitely looking forward to having a decent plot of land again.

I'm a total egg junkie, so buying eggs from the store, even an organic grocery chain, is totally killing me. I cannot wait to get chickens again!

5. Your experiences form the basis of *Get Your Pitchfork On!*, but you also did some research. Please tell us a bit about that experience.

The most interesting and reaffirming part of working on *Get Your Pitchfork On!* was the research I did. It helped to hear other people's stories and confirm that I was by no means alone in having experienced challenges as an urban transplant.

After we sold the farm, I called my Grandma Athens. She is also a writer, so I knew she would say yes when I asked if I could come and stay with her to work on my book. I spent four weeks over October and November 2009 in Appleton, Wisconsin, writing and researching. Appleton is right on the cusp of being a small city but is still, really, a large town, surrounded by farmland. So, I read the local paper and toured around with my aunts, who educated me in both family history and rural Midwestern life.

In the spring of 2010, I served as the writer-in-residence in an extremely rural county in Oregon: Harney. For two months, I traveled around the county (which is more than 10,000 square miles in size!) and taught writing to schoolchildren and adults, and also had a lot of time to work on the book. While I was there I interviewed a veterinarian, hiked with llamas and got an extensive lesson in firearms. One of the kids introduced me to her pigs. It was perfect to be re-immersed in a rural place while working on the book.

After I had a full draft, I sent it to people all over the United States for feedback—friends from North Carolina, Florida, Minnesota and of course Oregon —to make sure I hadn't missed anything and that it wasn't a Pacific Northwest-specific book.

6. Your obvious love of storytelling also plays into your artistic Etsy business, ithaka: repurposed literary ephemera. Does the concept of reusing paper play into the same values you had as a farmer?

That is an insightful question. I'd never thought about it, but you are absolutely right—no farmer I know lives an extravagant lifestyle. Frugality and thrift are valued, which is, incidentally, an interesting middle ground between farmers and city-environmentalists.

I have pretty much always been an "environmentalist." Part of the challenge of the artwork I create is that it has to come from a first-hand source. I only cut books that are damaged or obsolete, like encyclopedia volumes and atlases that include the Soviet Union. It would be easy to print images from the Internet or photocopy the books I have, but my goal is to take material out of the waste stream.

Also, I have to note that I was never a "farmer" per se. I often refer to the land and buildings we owned as a "farm," but my husband and I never sold our produce.

7. In addition to your new nonfiction book, you have published a lot of short fiction and creative nonfiction. Any advice for writers who are trying to get their work out there?

Start small—you can't get into [insert prestigious literary journal here] right out of the chute. If a publication offers writers' guidelines, for god's sake read them and follow the directions. Don't get "cute" in your cover letter; be sincere and concise. Good writing stands out far more than some kind of snarky attitude or clever typeface. (Can you tell I've been an editor before?) Send work that is appropriate for the publication. The best way to determine that is to read the publication.

Attend and then try to do local readings. If you're serious about being a writer, then you have to be a team player and go to writers' events. We all know it's all about you, but you have to at least pretend otherwise. Don't be competitive; we're all in this together.

Kristy's wordsmithing blog is kristyathens.com. Learn more about her book at getyourpitchforkon.com.

Julia Stoops:
Literary Fiction, Art, Web Design

Julia Stoops' creativity transcends form. She has earned acclaim in numerous fields, including visual art, teaching, website design and fiction writing.

Her first novel, *Parts Per Million*, is an intense, fast-paced journey through the lives of three eco-activists who run an underground media operation from their house in Southeast Portland. The delicate balance of power is disrupted when their young, well-meaning patron brings home a disheveled stranger he meets at the bus stop.

The writing is a heady blend of plot and specific details Julia collected through meticulous research. *Parts Per Million* uses three point-of-view characters —each activist has an original, distinctive voice—to create the realistic interior world of the seemingly mismatched roommates as they battle the injustices happening outside their front door.

Julia completed *Parts Per Million* in 2011. Her years of work on the manuscript were supported by an Oregon Arts Commission Fellowship in 2005 and a grant from the Pacific Northwest College of Art.

Julia, a New Zealand native and Portland, Oregon, resident since 1994, earned a bachelor's degree in visual art from the Corcoran College of Art, a bachelor's degree in philosophy from the University of Auckland and a master's degree in painting from Portland State University. She taught at the Pacific Northwest College of Art for more than a decade, and she has a twenty-five-year history of exhibiting her visual art.

In 2001, Julia founded her own company, Blue Mouse Monkey, specializing in branding and web design for changemakers. Since its inception, the business has thrived, building original sites for various foundations, nonprofits, research organizations, progressive businesses and creative professionals.

1. Tell us about your novel, *Parts Per Million.*

It's about a guy, John Nelson, who once worked for the Forest Service. He had a house, a wife, the usual middle-class deal. Then one day he had an epiphany and left it all to join a band of radical media activists.

That was years ago, and by the time the story opens in 2002, John Nelson still hasn't figured out whether he's done the right thing. He didn't envision saving the world would be so hard. His ideals remain strong, but the acts of sabotage have become tiresome. His fellow activists—young computer hacker Jen Owens and Vietnam vet Irving Fetzer—think he's a square. Their radio show can't compete with corporate media. And the Bush administration is growing scarier by the day.

The activists' household gets shaken up by the arrival of Deirdre, an Irish photographer with a secret drug problem. Maybe Nelson can't save the world, but he is going to try to save Deirdre.

As the country gears up for an unwanted war, Nelson, Jen and Fetzer's sleuthing uncovers war-technologies fraud and corruption at a local university. As they close in on the truth, they face escalating danger. Meanwhile, Deirdre's increasingly destructive behavior forces the compadres to confront their commitment to each other and the cause to which they have sacrificed "normal" lives.

Stepping back from the plot, *Parts Per Million* is also about not having control over your world: shit gets strange and you can't explain it. It's about democracy and freedom under threat during a difficult time in recent American history. It's about a subculture that is misunderstood, and even feared, yet wants nothing more than a free and fair existence for all. And it's also about enduring friendship and commitment and rising above adversity. And there's humor in the book, too! We read because we like to be absorbed in entertaining stories. I kept coming back to that key precept while I wrote this book.

2. Your book is rooted in a specific place and time, namely Portland, Oregon, in 2002. Why

there and then? How did your background in anti-war activism and alternative news radio play into your decision to write about this particular moment in history?

At that time I dove into anti-war activism and alternative news radio. There was so much to say about what was happening in our society. But after a while I became frustrated. It felt like preaching to the choir. Fiction, because of its entertainment value, seemed like a good alternative tactic.

In 2002, the U.S. built the false case for invading Iraq. It was also the year the government rolled out Homeland Security, Operation TIPS and Total Information Awareness. Ordinary people really were being thrown out of shopping malls for wearing peace T-shirts and detained by authorities for requesting non-flag stamps at the post office. It was a crazy, messed-up time. I wanted to depict that time through complex characters as they grappled with the everyday experience of absurdity and anxiety.

3. In *Parts Per Million*, you convey many technical details with great authority—and without slowing the plot down. What kind of research did you do? Was it an ongoing effort throughout your drafts, or did you compile facts first, then write?

I did different kinds of research. For instance, every word the characters read in a newspaper or hear on the TV is verbatim from news reports at that time. I have VHS tapes, news clippings, magazines and so many digital files you wouldn't believe. I'm glad I captured what I could, because some of it I can't find on the Internet now.

Then there were the points I got help with—for instance, the computer security details. I admire Jen's hacking prowess, but it's a talent I unfortunately do not share. A couple of computer security guys were kind enough to help me with the hacking scenes. I had the scenes blocked out already—I knew how they fit into the plot—but the actual blow-by-blow details came from experts.

Jen also gets arrested. I haven't been arrested in Portland during an anti-war demonstration, but I got details from a woman who was. We met up through Indymedia: She put a call out for a video-tape of her arrest, and I happened to have her arrest on tape, because I was in the habit of bringing a camera to demonstrations. I gave her the video and she let me interview her. Most of the juicy material, like how pitch dark and disorienting the police wagon was, didn't make it to the final draft, but the snippets that remain are authentic.

The real challenge was not getting the material—it was editing down what I had. When you've gone to a lot of trouble to find out exactly how something works, it takes restraint to pare that information down to just-enough-to-make-it-believable.

4. In your novel, there are three point-of-view characters. When in your writing process did you decide to tell the story that way? What was challenging about your choice?

The point of view characters are Nelson, Jen and Fetzer, the three media activists who live together. Getting there took several iterations. Originally the novel was all omniscient third person, because that was the only way I knew how to write. I hadn't studied creative writing or literature in college, so from a craft perspective I was ignorant of alternatives.

Then I joined Stevan Allred and Joanna Rose's critique group. They opened my eyes to the possibilities of writing not only in point of view, but in voice. That was a revelation, and I had fun playing with the characters in new ways.

At first there were five voices: Deirdre had a say, and so did Franky, the trust-fund kid who helps the media group out. Franky is sweet but not too bright. I struggled to render him authentically and later dropped his POV. So I was down to four: the three activists and Deirdre. And the novel stayed with four voices through a couple more drafts.

Then it became clear that the novel was way too long. As Stevan said, "You haven't written a novel, you've written a mini-series." I had to make massive cuts to bring it down to a typical novel size. Many subplots got the axe, as did some characters' back stories. Scenes were cut. And Deirdre's POV was cut. That was the hardest decision to make. I grieved when I cut her voice out of the novel. It was the most poetic and beautiful of the voices, and she noticed things the other characters took for granted. But the clincher was that her interior drama was so big and so sad that it was dominating the story. And it's Nelson's story. Deirdre's purpose as a character is to wring him out and change him. It wasn't appropriate for her to upstage him.

So I settled on three alternating voices, and that's the final form of the novel.

5. Julia, you've created some art featuring John Nelson, your protagonist. What medium did you use? Did portraying Nelson in a visual way change your relationship to him on the page?

John Nelson is an everyman figure: average build, average height, average clothes. He's sensitive, and burdened with the weight of the world, and when he experiences tragedy it's transformative, allowing him to find his true role in life. As a visual artist, it was a natural avenue of exploration for me to depict Nelson visually. He's in several small acrylic and oil paintings from 2003 and 2004-06.

He and his compadres dominated my imagination for years. I don't think working on the paintings changed my relationship to him on the page, but it let me explore him in another dimension. You can see the paintings at juliastoops.net, under "The Things in the Sky" and "As a Young Man."

6. Along with bringing *Parts Per Million* to your writing group, you hand-picked a few readers in various fields to offer feedback. Please tell us about that process and how those extra sets of eyes shaped your manuscript revisions.

The weekly critique group was fantastic at

helping me with the craft of the sentence. I learned so much at Stevan and Joanna's table, and the book would simply not exist without their steady guidance over the years.

The later handpicked readers, to whom I will be ever grateful, were a great complement to the critique group. They came from different backgrounds and read the whole novel at once. I think it's important to not rely solely on other writers to critique your work. Non-writers will be smart and perceptive about a novel in a whole different way. The readers I chose represented a cross-section of the book's ideal audiences, and so their advice, usually on the level of larger patterns and themes, helped shape the book on a different scale.

The weekly critique group helped me craft each brick and build structures. The later readers told me whether the structures were well-balanced and intuitive to move through. Additionally, after making those massive cuts, it was the readers with fresh eyes who told me where I needed to restore crucial information.

7. How do you balance writing and working as a creative professional in the web design industry? When do you find time to write?

Hahahahaha! That's a trick question, right? But seriously, it's taken a lot of discipline to work through the novel's drafts while transitioning out of my teaching career and growing a small business. I write in spurts. And I'll admit there have been periods of weeks, sometimes months, without writing. My web-design work involves a lot of sitting at a computer and problem-solving. Writing also entails sitting at a computer and problem-solving. (Extended handwriting is almost impossible now due to tendonitis.) Sometimes I'm all used up at the end of a day. But other times I'm not. I guess there were enough of those other times over the last ten years for me to get this novel finished!

Learn more about Julia's novel, Parts Per Million, *at partspermillion.net. Her art site is juliastoops.net and the Blue Mouse Monkey site is bluemousemonkey.com.*

Flash Essays
on Who,
What,
When,
Where,
Why
and
How
We Write

Shiny Object, Shiny Object
By Kate Gray

On too many days I'll do everything, except write: slide a stray hair through the dust on my desk, rearrange files, track down an unanswered email. But some days I have some strategies to foil myself:

Get some of the buggers done.
Even if just a few, get some off your back, the naggiest.

Walk away.
Isolate. Go into sensory deprivation in the basement or in a remote, rural area. Without music or TV or licking dogs too close, but with wind through Ponderosa Pine, the sound of approaching trains.

Set a time limit.
Two hours is a really good stretch. I can focus for that long, although sometimes I have to build up to it. The joy is finding two hours too little time.

Turn off email notification.
It's too easy to see the shiny number in the red circle.

Turn on music.
I can't have words. For a while R. Carlos Nakai,

the *Canyon Trilogy*, worked magic, and immediately the sad mountain light of the Navajo lands flooded me, and the poems would stick with pain.

Exercise long and slow.

Long, slow distance intoxicates. After an hour on a bike, after the focus on one-foot-two-feet, spin-spin-spin, everything else falls away. And I am balance and shift and friction. I am not papers-to-grade or garbage-night or groceries. Sometimes I am metaphor and a character's motivation and what-happens-next.

Create deadlines.

Join a weekly or monthly group. Find your Catholic (i.e., guilt) if you show up without something in hand.

Beat the rush.

Wake up early, when you're in that almost dreaming/almost awake place.

May you find what works for you. May you do your work. I'm eager to read it.

Kate Gray tends her students' stories. Her first full-length book of poems, Another Sunset We Survive, *was a finalist for the Oregon Book Award (2007) and followed chapbooks* Bone-Knowing *(Gertrude Poetry Prize, 2006) and* Where She Goes *(Blue Light Chapbook Prize, 2000). Her unpublished novel,* Skin Drag, *looks at bullying without blinking.*

Because I Like the Letters
By Stevan Allred

I once heard Charles D'Ambrosio, a writer known for his collection of typewriters, tell an audience he loved all the tools of writing except the hammer and chisel. I have gone from being a six-year-old with a fat pencil in his hand struggling to make the letter 'a' to a sixty-year-old with word processors in three different rooms of my home. I love my keyboards. I love my pencils. I love my Lamy pens.

In my writing life I have written novels, stories, essays, poems and zines. It was while I was producing the first of my zines, *Dixon Ticonderoga*, a hand-lettered homage to pencils, that the pleasure of printing words by hand finally made sense to me. Working at my kitchen table at 4 a.m., pencil in hand, happily and methodically forming letters, I understood this: letters make words, words make sentences, sentences make paragraphs, paragraphs make stories. And stories make meaning.

Writing is a physical act. It is manual labor, a thing we do with our hands, a labor of love that cricks our necks and strains our shoulders. Like the painter who said he painted because he liked the smell of paint, I write because I like the feel of my Lamy pen in my hand, because I like the touch of the keyboard beneath my fingers, because I like the letters and words appearing on the screen or the page. I write stories because stories are how I make sense of my life. I love the writing of them because I love every jot and tittle of punctuation, and the making of every letter, of every word.

Stevan Allred has survived circumcision, a tonsillectomy, a religious upbringing, the '60s, the War on Poverty, the break-up of The Beatles, any number of bad haircuts, years of psychotherapy, the Reagan Revolution, the War on Drugs, the Roaring '90s, plantar fasciitis, the Lewinsky Affair, the Internet bubble, the Florida recount of 2000, the Bush Oughts, the War on Terror, teen-aged children, a divorce, hay fever, the real estate bubble, male pattern baldness and heartburn. His work has appeared in numerous literary journals and websites, and he has twice been nominated for a Pushcart Prize.

Brave on the Page

By Kristen Forbes

My writing comes from a place of terror and inadequacy. A few of the fears and insecurities that rattle in my brain on a regular basis: I'm afraid of death (and sometimes life). I'm afraid of failure (and also success). I'm afraid of pushing myself forward (but stagnation, too). I'm afraid of the idea that I may never fully know someone. I'm afraid that no one may ever fully know me. I'm afraid of silly things: technology and gossip. I'm afraid of bigger things: aging and loneliness. I'm frequently afraid of the world. I'm often afraid of myself.

On the page, I don't just write my own endings—I write my own beginnings and middles, too. I'm not at the mercy of things beyond my control; I'm allowed to tell whatever story I want to tell, unconfined by the paralyzing thoughts that plague me in real life. My fictional characters are braver than I'll ever be. The "me" in my personal essays is an electrified, badass version of myself whose ability to observe things in hindsight is only possible because the weaker, terrified version of me dutifully took notes while quietly avoiding the action. As a writer, I have the ability to pull the covers over my head and hide under my bed—and, while I'm there, I can craft a story about a girl who is boldly living her life.

Author Willy Vlautin often refers to writing as

his friend: dependable, comforting, forgiving. In my stories, the girl might actually get the guy. Better yet, if she doesn't get the guy, she can win the sympathy of her audience. She is heard. She is understood. She is loved.

My writing comes from a place of cowardice, but I allow myself the luxury of feeling brave while doing it.

Kristen Forbes is a freelance writer whose work has been published or is forthcoming from Crack the Spine Literary Magazine, Constellations: A Journal of Poetry and Fiction, Front Porch Review, Bartleby Snopes *(where her short story was voted the July 2012 Story of the Month),* Down in the Dirt Magazine, Portland Tribune, *the Stand up to Cancer website and other publications. She holds a BFA in writing, literature and publishing from Emerson College and an MFA in creative writing from Antioch University. She writes at krissymick.blogspot.com.*

Why I Write Out Loud
By Robert Hill

This sentence that you're reading, with its flexible, conversational structure and its texture and its run-on length that would probably give Raymond Carver fits, reads the way that it does because as I wrote it, I spoke it out loud. I write all my sentences out loud. I need to hear the cadence to know how to stack one word up against the next, and I need the aural beat of every stacked word to help me understand where the sentence wants to go. Once a sentence is running at a pace that sounds good to me and leading to another and a third and more and more, I read them all back, over and over, from the start to wherever I've left off, because the momentum I've set will take the paragraph on its own journey to where it needs to land, and where that is is often a place I would not have gotten to unless I said it all out loud.

I grew up on stories told at bedtime, told on car trips, told at the dinner table after dessert. My mother told these stories, five or six of them, over and over in rotation, like reruns of "I Love Lucy" that I never tired of hearing. A few of my favorites: the same wagon train tale told at bedtime in which I was the baby, and always, always, falling out of the wagon and being left behind. Or the story of her trip to Europe in 1950, the first year commercial travel opened up after the war, of the boat being full of nuns because it was Holy Year, about her luggage being lost for three weeks, about her and her two friends hitching a ride with a Pernod-swigging Argentinean who stuffed them into a Renault and drove them over the top of the Swiss Alps at night because she was too drunk to see the turn-off for the tunnel. Every syllable of these words told in my mother's raconteur's voice full of wit and Brooklyn inflection I loved hearing, every entertaining sentence told again made the usual silence of our family bearable, and as long as they were retold from the beginning, dinner after dinner, bedtime after bedtime, vacation drive after vacation drive, no matter that I'd heard them all before, hearing them again out loud from the beginning to wherever our lives left off left in me a sense that one day I'd have my own narrative to tell, and it would be one that I'd have to hear out loud first to complete.

Robert Hill is the author of the novels When All Is Said and Done, *which was a finalist for the Oregon Book Award, and the forthcoming* The Remnants. *A grant writer by day, he is currently at work on a new novel.*

Where
By Liz Scott

Even as a kid I needed noise. Homework in front of the TV, reading with the radio or record player on, studying on the school bus. Maybe it was imprinting from my earliest crib-bound days when we lived in the old lower east side, not the too-cool-for-the-room place it is now, but the one with police sirens and gun shots. Quiet is too quiet for me. I can't think. So, it's easiest to write in the summer. Bear with me here. I live in an urban setting partly because I want to walk to what I need as much as possible. Since I like noise, I like to write in cafes, therefore I want to carry my laptop to a cafe, therefore it's more pleasant to do that when the weather cooperates. I live in Portland, Oregon, now so weather cooperating is a semi-rare occurrence. I'm like a moon flower, writing-wise. I produce one season a year and then slam shut.

It's summer now and I cart my laptop to one of the three or four cafes nearby because, again, I live in Portland, Oregon, and you can't swing a cat in this town without hitting a coffee shop. In fact, yesterday I was working at my local Peet's during the mid-afternoon rush and these two people were talking and one said something like, "She sucks air like a jet engine…" and I thought, Cool, I'm going to use that.

It's morning now and I'm home. But the doors are open, the trash trucks are doing their thing, rush hour is in full swing and someone's on the way to the hospital.

Liz Scott: psychologist, reader, writer, ex-New Yorker, Francophile, movie freak, published short storyist, over-the-moon nonna, political junkie, rock star wannabe.

Move

By Jackie Shannon Hollis

Perfect sentences come to me when I'm out walking. I'm not intending it or waiting for it, but something about the steady pace, the absence of doing-ness, seems to draw things up: the start of a story, a way of saying something I'd been reaching for, a connection of all the ideas in a piece I'm working on. If I'm lucky, I've brought paper and pencil. I don't always, so I try to hold on to that perfect sentence and when I come home, I take up paper and pencil and I write that sentence, and there is a wonderful flow that comes in these moments, and one sentence leads to another.

Those perfect sentences come when I'm driving, too. I used to try to record these, but I didn't like it. Something was lost. Plus, it seemed a little dangerous trying to find the record button. If I'm driving alone, and no one is waiting for me, I pull over and write it down. Long waits at stoplights are nice, too. I never complain about these. I scribble notes on Post-Its.

Once, I mapped out a whole story on a drive from Condon, my hometown on the east side of Oregon, back to Portland, on the west side. I knew I'd remember it and I smiled and followed I-84 along the Columbia River, as one thing and another came. That story, "Swim," was inspired by all that water.

Though the real hands-on labor of writing comes when I spend hours at my desk with my computer,

I've always counted movement as a place of writing for me. If I'm stuck on a piece, I put it in my second-attention. I go fold laundry or pull weeds and dead-head flowers in my garden. I go get the mail or go for a longer walk. Sometimes I lie down on the floor and stretch. All these things help me reach; they help me breathe. Stories need movement and air. I trust my second-attention to keep working. I've got to move to get where the story needs to go.

Jackie Shannon Hollis' short stories and essays have appeared in a variety of literary journals including The Sun, Rosebud, Inkwell, High Desert Journal *and* Slice. *She lives west of Portland in a place her friends call the Tree House, for all the cedars swaying out back. She has completed a novel and is now working on a memoir.*

Running Commentary
By Nancy Townsley

I write on the run.

Out on the open road, I'm able to see life closer up than I would otherwise, from a position that puts me right next to the swelling Willamette River in March and the dusty-hot Forest Park trails in July and the golden cornstalks of Sauvie Island in September. Running allows me to crouch down in the dirt and sift through it, to wonder about all the gritty, messy layers of life I want to pretend aren't there but *are* there anyway, playing footsie with my sense of security, sticking their tongues out at my hope that, for this one solitary day at least, I'll mostly be all right.

I write about all of this in my head when I'm running, something that riding in a car, or on public transportation, would never allow me to do. There's too much noise, too many distractions. On the MAX train I might notice all kinds of wonderful things: the just-right pale blue color of the flower attached to an old woman's felt hat, or the odd way the teenager with eyebrow piercings and dark eye make-up sneered at the bus driver just now, as if he were planning to come back later and murder him while the driver is sucking down his bologna-and-cheese sandwich and a cup of Dunkin' Donuts coffee.

But I'm definitely neurotic enough that I'd forget to write any of them down. There'd be meals to plan, bills to pay, love to make, Facebook posts to catch up on. It just wouldn't work. So I do it on the run, an act that has provided me a Yellow Brick Road leading home to the sanctuary of self-expression.

Writing, my many-times-spurned but always hopeful lover, has stalked me for much of my life, through years of game-playing and explosive, short-lived attempts at real relationship. It has followed me around, tiptoeing, like Peter Pan's mischievous shadow, until I finally turned toward it and said, in fake resignation, "Okay, writing, you've got me. I love you and will never leave you again." I've discovered that in order to write well you need to write often, and that sometimes the mere act of it reaches out and boxes your ears—but if you're brave enough to face the pain you almost always eventually get to this place of real blessing.

Running and writing, and before that, each one separately, have kept me from losing my mind more than once, and I expect that before I'm done, they will again, probably many more times than I can imagine as I sit here today, spilling words onto paper, my panting yellow dog by my side, exhausted but satisfied after a rollicking run we completed together just an hour or so ago.

Nancy Townsley lives in a quirky 1926 farmhouse two miles from the mighty Columbia River in St. Helens, Oregon. She has been a journalist since the Me Decade, a writer since forever and a runner since 1998, and she is working on a book of essays about writing and running.

Add Real Stuff to Your Fiction
By Sherri H. Hoffman

In the real world, we're always mashing up against the concrete objects that fill our lives, commonplace things—teapot, hairbrush, pencil, shoe. Added to story, these objects make the fictional world accessible and relevant. "Stuff" defines setting and character, and intimates status or desires and the very recognizable human need to document our own existence. Consider the following:

See Dick. See Jane.

Or:
See Dick in his pimpin' white fedora and Jane on his arm rocking the red stilettos.

Or this:
See Dick hunkered down against the wind on Second and Burnside in a second-hand wool coat, the Goodwill tag sticking out at the collar. See Jane drive by in her pink Cadillac, her hair a perfect coif tied up in a leopard-print bandana. She doesn't wave.

All the greats knew how to use real stuff: T.S. Eliot grasped a handful of dust; Raymond Carver gave us birthday cake, peacocks, flying buttresses, a blind man's cane; Hemingway's Robert Cohn rejected sliced cucumbers for pickled herring.

Objects often carry great weight on multiple levels, which serves to deepen character, authenticate setting, increase tension and become metaphor. In order to do so, the objects must be specific and accurate. At an airport security checkpoint, the Maasai woman from Kenya isn't likely to have mascara tubes and liposuction pamphlets spill from her tipped purse, and it's doubtful the blonde from San Diego in line behind her is returning to her house made of cow dung. Although the reverse could be intriguing.

They're all around—regular objects poised and ready to be swept into the fictional world. A martini glass imprinted with peach lipstick. A baby's blue shoe. Snatch them up. Identify, name and infuse your writing with real-world stuff.

Sherri H. Hoffman is a working writer, social media nerd and sports fanatic currently pursuing an MFA at Pacific University and a novel. Some of her stories appear in PANK, Etchings, *the* Salmon Creek Journal, Duck & Herring Magazine, *and various online publications. When not writing, she's been spotted hiking in the Northwest forests or fishing from a canoe. Read more:* sherrihhoffman.com.

Pen and Paper
By Steve Denniston

I always carry a ball-point pen in one back pocket and a piece of paper in my other back pocket. It makes it easy to write down ideas I get or lines of dialogue I hear. Like the time my brother-in-law was telling a story about growing up and said, "That was back in '83 or some stupid year like that." Browsing through my notes later, I read that line and found a place for it in a scene I was working on.

At work, sometimes in the middle of class, I scribble down a note. Once a third grade boy admitted he ate a bite of dog food. I asked, "What's it taste like?" He thought about it, took his time and finally said, "Cat food." I loved that kid and loved his answer so much I wrote it down and it inspired a whole chapter in my novel.

My church has been an endless source of material. Recently at coffee hour I overheard someone say, "That gun I bought last month? That thing shoots better than I do." I wrote that down because I instantly knew which of my characters would say it and even the chapter it belonged in.

Later, during a break at Bible study, a man I barely knew showed me pictures of his grandkids on his phone. He began crying and told me he's leaving his girlfriend because she's married, and he knows how wrong that is, and he loves her so much it's the hardest thing he's ever done. His pain is so raw and honest, it overwhelms both of us and I wonder how to get all of that on the page while questioning whether I should even try. It's his story and his pain and I should have the decency to simply be present with him in that room. I have a pen in one pocket, the paper in another, and when he's done crying and we're back with the group, I don't write anything down because I'll never forget that moment.

You can follow Steve by finding him in Southeast Portland (check coffee shops first, then the bars) or on Twitter: @SteveDenniston.

When I Am in My Write Mind
By Harold L. Johnson

When I am in my write mind it's August before sunrise and the moon is a crescent of morning cantaloupe under Venus and Jupiter

When I am in my write mind I'm deep in the water checking out huge scaly fish named Geoffrey, Edmund, Bill

When I am in my write mind I'm doing that dream thing through space to the violins of the Sixth Brandenburg Concerto to meet Thelonious at 52nd Street

When I am in my write mind there's a bright golden haze on the meadow, and it ain't in Oklahoma

When I am in my write mind it's that day in the bare living room, done with *War and Peace,* hitching up my pants, I stare out through the blinds and, because I'm out of my mind eighteen, think maybe someday I could…

When I am in my write mind and turn from the wreckage behind me to the horizon, I understand I can dig it as ore

When I am in my write mind after Cheerios, coffee and Krugman, I'm ready again like the day before and the day before that, having a time among the streaming vowels, looking in the end to be covered only with earth

When I am in my write mind the big dog in my dreams looks like a friendly bear, rubs against my shins and tells me his name is Bruno

When I am in my write mind there is only one thing to do

Harold L. Johnson was born in the Yakima Valley during the heart of The Great Depression. Since college, he has taught, played tennis and written in Portland. His work has appeared in numerous regional journals and anthologies. He is married to the artist Anne Griffin Johnson.

Fish Lake, Yo
By Bart King

I'm a writer because I'm a reader.

But I'm not one of those insufferable twits whose constant thought while reading is, "Man, I could do better than THAT."

I'm a *different* kind of insufferable twit, the kind with a running commentary in his head. Maybe I disagree with my reading material and a counter-punch is forming in my mind. Perhaps I want to know more about my subject and the ensuing research leads to my writing something-something.

For example, a week or so ago, I read an article titled "Man Texts, 'I Need To Quit Texting' Before Driving Off Cliff." This led me to do some research on the statistics behind multi-tasking behind the wheel... and I was able to sell the piece to an education publisher in short order. So yeah, reading can be nice work, if you can get it.

Of course, reading isn't the sole source of my writing ideas. Conversations and quiet moments also yield bounty. For instance, I was out for a solitary hike this week at Fish Lake. Yes, it's a real lake right here in Oregon. You can imagine how the naming process went.

Trapper (gazing out at the water): This unnamed lake sure is purty.

Settler: But it needs its own moniker. Let's brainstorm! And remember, no idea is a bad idea.

Trapper: How about Water Lake? No—Wet Lake! Or maybe Highly Moist Lake?

[pause]

Settler: You've been alone up in these mountains a long time, haven't you?

Anyway, while I was hiking near Fish Lake, two thoughts came to me:

1) A cool name for a novel would be *My Dad Can Kill Your Dad*.

2) Some sugarless gum would taste good right about now.

I'm pretty sure I can do something with one of those ideas. Anyway, before I go, let me share some Writerly Advice: When reading spurs a train of thought, it is usually one that is easily derailed.

So always go offline when you write. Now if you'll excuse me, I need to check my email.

Bart King writes funny books for middle readers and immature adults. A middle-school teacher for fifteen years, he has more than a half-million books in print, and his work has been translated into Chinese, Spanish and Australian. Bart prefers to be thought of as a "non-award winning author" despite some small evidence to the contrary.

Mentor

By Gigi Little

Mr. Mulloney gave me an A on my paper. I wrote about wanting to be a writer. I'd always wanted to be a writer, a little, but when Mr. Mulloney told me I could, I really wanted it.

I was a sophomore in high school with no friends except for the girl who pretended she believed she came from the planet X-Squared, and Mr. Mulloney was my English teacher. He was also writing a novel.

He said, "Your ideas are original and clever."

He said, "You're mature way beyond your years."

I felt original and clever. I felt mature way beyond my years. I felt I could be a writer.

The next year, when he was no longer my teacher, we became friends. He'd confide in me about his rejection letters, his worry that students didn't take him seriously, that women didn't take him seriously, since he was five-foot-two. We didn't talk about me, but that was all right because he thought I could be a writer.

Ring of the phone, his voice in my ear, high, almost feminine: "Can I share something?"

It wasn't really sharing since he'd only called to read me a story he'd written, and he didn't really want to know what I thought unless I loved it.

Sometimes I didn't, but I hated to disappoint people.

Ring of the doorbell: Mr. M. with a stack of new writing to show off.

We sat on the couch. He sat too close.

Inside, I was first person wishing to be third, to be outside myself, away.

I could tell he had a crush on me, that he hoped someday to be more than my mentor, and I felt guilty not liking him back.

But his crush also made me think maybe I'd get published. Maybe I'd get what I wanted. Because his crush sprang from my talent, from my love of writing, from our shared obsession. His crush sprang from all the things that would make me a real writer someday.

I was pretty sure.

Unless it was just a crush.

Gigi Little's work has appeared in the books Portland Noir, The Pacific Northwest Reader *and* The Frozen Moment, *as well as literary magazines. By day, she works as Lead Visual Merchandiser for Powell's Books in Portland, Oregon. Before moving to Portland, Gigi spent fifteen years in the circus business as a lighting director and professional circus clown, and she can spin a mean lasso.*

Making Feral Creatures
By Tammy Lynne Stoner

Sometimes folks who want to be writers ask, "How do I write?" Then they are told many things: don't use adverbs; write only in first person; talk in common, street language. But, as my great-great grandmother might have said if I'd ever met her, "The only way to know your gin isn't poison is to make it yourself."

To create art (not just story), go into The Cave by yourself. Be brave enough to write in the dark without other people's opinions until you feel you've found your voice. Start by writing a painful moment from your life—detail by detail. Start by writing a sci-fi tale about water. Start by writing a letter to the person who broke your heart when you were five.

This might take years. It took me years.

Eventually you'll find your voice. You'll pop your filthy cavehead into the sunlight like a groundhog on smack, and in your bone-thin fist will be the feral creature that is your first manuscript.

Now, you know, you must leave The Cave and tame your feral beast.

This is when other voices come in. These other voices are sometimes called "craft" or "editor" or "the douchebag in my writing group." They will help you see places where you can slow down the writing or spots where the narrative logic is missing.

They will praise what is brilliant. They may even help you bury your beloved work—as I have many a time—when there is nothing more that can be done to save it.

You will appreciate and love these voices, even the douchebag (maybe especially the douchebag). But, since you've done time in The Cave, you won't grow dependent on these voices. You can trust your own opinion. You will know that craft can show you how to edit your creation, but not how to be a writer because you already are a writer—you became that in The Cave when no one was looking.

Tammy Lynne Stoner is a writer, artist and Fiction Editor of Gertrude Journal. *She has been nominated for a Million Writers Award, was offered a Summer Literary Seminar fellowship, has been published more than a dozen times, and in 2012, had one of her paintings selected for the cover of the* New England Review. *Tammy is also the writer/creator of "Dottie's Magic Pockets," a kids' show for modern families that has played at a dozen international film festivals and is available in more than one hundred libraries. On the side, she panics about the twins she and her ladyfriend are having soon—very soon!*

Pinewood Table

By Joanna Rose

My yard is a mess—
Oregon grape, Johnson grass,
coral bells, buttercups,
kitchen chairs, garden tools,
empty bird feeders,
empty terra cotta pots.

My house is old—
old windows, no drapes, dusty floors,
no rugs, big empty rooms,
no one else here,
a black and white feral cat
and the Sunday *New York Times*
on the porch.

But there is a soft gray place,
with happy tangles of neurons,
and the sound in there is sing song la la,
eye rhymes, and false parallels, where poem
is poem and story tells, tickle my fancy,
float my boat, and synapses fire
like Fourth of July into gifts
of early rain, four in the morning
sparrow song, funerals of no one I know,
Gorecki's Third Symphony,
and any memory
of Iowa in summer.

Joanna Rose is a novelist and poet and writer of stories. She teaches young writers and hangs out in classrooms with other writers who do the same. She lives near a park in Southeast Portland, in a small blue house, which is home to the Pinewood Table critique group.

Wherever I Am
By Emma Burcart

I used to write at home. Usually in my pajamas, steps away from the coffee pot and my own bathroom. There are plenty of people who write at the library, at coffee shops and even on the MAX while they commute to work. I was never one of them.

When I decided to take writing seriously, I set up the space it deserved. A desk for my computer, a separate table for the printer and a giant cushy chair. I kept the curtains drawn tight and let the darkness bring the stories alive.

Becoming a homeowner made me even pickier. I had a whole room just for writing. I spent weeks setting it up. Orange walls, a silver ceiling and one accent wall with beautiful black and white damask wallpaper straight from the home decor magazines. It was a thing of beauty.

I finished one novel and started another in that room. I began blogging and dabbled in magazine writing. In that beautiful orange room, I have grown as a writer, as a woman and as a person.

So when the time came to leave Oregon, I was worried. Would I be able to write somewhere new? The space held magical power for me and I was afraid my writing was tied to it.

I've never been so happy to be wrong. Location may be everything when it comes to real estate, but writing is bigger than that. Since I've been away from Oregon and my beautiful space, I've learned to write wherever I am. Sometimes that's in the quiet dining room at my best friend's house while her baby and husband sleep in the recliner five feet away. Other times it's the Starbucks down the street or the cute French restaurant in the fancy part of town. Times like that I may drink too much coffee or eat way too much cheese. But the writing never suffers. I put on my headphones and the rest of the world disappears.

It doesn't matter where I am, the words find me.

Emma Burcart lived most of her life in Portland, Oregon. She fell in love with writing in a class for elementary teachers and never stopped. Her first love is fiction, but she also enjoys essays, creative nonfiction and blogging about girlie things. She recently decided to move to Miami, but when she stopped in Raleigh, North Carolina, it felt like home, so she decided to stay for a while. You can find her somewhere on the highway with everything she owns in her car or blogging about her occasional epiphanies at emmaburcart.com.

Starbucks and Sensibility:
A Love Story
By Nicole Marie Schreiber

"It is a truth universally acknowledged that a writer in possession of children and a day job must be in want of a perfect place to write."

My Dearest Starbucks:

I am writing this letter as a token of my love, affection and devotion to you. 'Tis not your tall nonfat chai frappuccinos with whip, your dark chocolate graham crackers, your grande tea lattes nor your sugared almonds that have captured my sensibilities (though all are quite delightful to the tongue).

I am addicted to you as a place for me to write—away from PlayMobil spy missions, Lego landmines, bickering children, mounds of laundry and a Labrador that keeps stealing shoes.

You have been my savior for the past two years, since I received my first gift card for Christmas upon my return to teaching. Seeing your name meant only one thing to me—creative freedom. When I was too distracted right after work and too tired later in the evening to even think about my manuscript, and with no money to go to retreats or conferences for inspiration, *you* were there for me.

Soon, the smell of coffee beans meant new words on the page. I tried to make my time with you last, buying the least expensive drink on the menu that I liked (tall Awake tea). I soon discovered that your gift cards are very popular with parents. The writer in me collected and relished each card I received, and when family found out about our affair, instead of having an intervention, they enabled me with more cards for you.

My beloved, whether we rendezvous at 5:30 a.m. or on a day off, you have given me more pages that I could ever dream of completing. I pray our affair lasts, and it is with my most sincere regard that I shall ever humbly bow before you, and be known to all as your loving servant in word scratchery...

Nicole Marie Schreiber

Nicole Marie Schreiber strives to write stories that create a sense of wonder. She holds an MFA in Writing for Children and Young Adults from the Vermont College of Fine Arts and has won numerous awards for her picture book, middle grade and poetry manuscripts. She is working on a historical middle grade novel and various picture books. When she is not writing at Starbucks, she can be found assisting her magician husband, reenacting favorite time periods with her two sons (late 18th century and the Renaissance are the current favorites), or sharing her love of reading with preschoolers. She is a member of the Portland-based critique group, Viva Scriva (vivascriva.com), and writes for their group blog as well as for her own at nicolemarieschreiber.wordpress.com.

Dialogue for Dollhouse People
By Amber Krieger

After my daughter was born, I thought where I'd write would be in my head, during those long hours nursing her to sleep and waiting for her to go limp enough to extract my nipple from her mouth without shocking her back awake. Hours in the waning summer daylight, and even more hours in the winter dark of our bedroom. The perfect place to listen for those opening lines, those bursts of voice in my head that have always signaled the start of a new story. To quietly observe the characters of the novel I began just before she was born.

This is not what happened. Most nights I lay there with my eyes open, thinking about the only thing my brain could focus on: babies. Instead of crafting dialogue, I rehearsed conversations I wanted to have with my husband—about our baby—should we ever find ourselves in the same room. I composed perfect Facebook statuses about my baby's chubby arms or how many pieces my heart burst into every time I watched her sleep. I made lists of things I wanted to write down in her first year diary.

Even these would leave my brain the moment I left the room.

After two years, the hormones wore off and the words came back. And it's not just dialogue for dollhouse people. There are no more long nursing sessions. But there is my one precious writing night. And there are little scraps of paper, stowed in pockets, and a green notebook carried in my purse. There are car naps—on errands I make up to get one hour of tapping on my laptop—and stroller naps where I pull over in the shade on Mount Tabor and scribble as fast as I can until I hear, "Mama, I see a resewah."

Amber Krieger's prize-winning short fiction has appeared in Carve Magazine, *the* Adirondack Review, cream city review, elimae *and elsewhere.*

Overnight

By Laura Stanfill

I lie on a twin bed squeezed against my long-limbed daughter, who insists on too many stuffed animals. I tell her to go to sleep, so I can go to France. As she sings songs to herself, I imagine men in a Vosges Valley village making music boxes. Whether what they drink is cold. How their nineteenth-century French words sound. My daughter touches my cheek. I fake sleep and think about calluses on the craftsmen's hands, and on their lace-making wives' hands, and on the hands of their children, who already know how to work. My daughter moves from songs to stories, from stories to slowed-down breaths. I lie there, eyes shut, until the story inside me gets restless. I must write one thing down. I get up. She wakes up. I lie down. We begin again.

The boy in my novel gets diagnosed with a weak constitution, and he believes what the doctor says. He stays in bed. He reads and rests. He wishes. My daughter rolls over, tilts her chin up, breathes deep. She started kindergarten this fall. The shift of her world has begun. Someday both my girls will leave this house without me. They will be broken apart by small things. I tell stories about brushing teeth, drinking milk, getting enough sleep, instead of filling pages with lace and music. Someday my girls will choose whether or not to be good to their bodies.

I am in my own bed, not in France, not at school, when the baby wakes. I change her diaper and latch her on. It's four o'clock when she falls back asleep, the time before the day begins, dark and quiet except for the thump of the paper against our front door. I make coffee. I leave the news outside. I go to France.

Laura Stanfill—novelist, award-winning journalist, freelance editor, knitter and Vassar graduate—believes in community. She is the founder of Forest Avenue Press and the editor of Brave on the Page, *which is based on her blog's Seven Questions interview series. Her website is laurastanfill.com.*

How I Write
By Kristi Wallace Knight

I.

In the shower, I think about my story. As hairs gleefully escape the tethers of my scalp and flee down the drain, little inspirations enter through my follicles. I know something new about my character! I have a terrible obstacle for her, and I know how she will overcome it!

I exit the shower, laughing rapturously, imagining myself writing as I mindlessly comb what's left of my hair.

II.

I Sit Before My Computer. No one can see me. I must tell Twitter that I #amwriting. Whew, that's better. Now, what was that idea again? Oh, that was my idea? That's dumb. I Will Now Write Something Even Better. With A First Sentence So Grand That Hemingway Would Fall To His Knees In Awe. As Soon As I Get More Coffee.

III.

Okay, I really mean it now. I'm going to write this scene. Or maybe it's not a scene, just, you know, some notes. That will help me write this totally awe-some scene when I have more time.

IV.

Maybe I should start a new book. I think I've tapped this one out.

V.

Okay, I've got forty-five minutes. I'll write a real-ly crappy version of this scene and fix it later. Wait, how does this scene fit into the story again? Do I even want that secondary character? Maybe I should kill her off. Or just strike out every reference of her from the beginning to here. Oh shit, now I've got fifteen minutes. Okay, well, I'll just free write. About how I'm not writing.

VI.

While making "ants on a log" for the after-school snack, inspiration strikes! Again! "Here, child, eat your ants and drink your milk and watch your cartoon, I'll be back in twenty-two minutes!"

One gorgeous sentence. Another astonishing sentence. A profound experience. Oh, I'm so in love with these characters, how could I have forsaken them? A beautiful insight. Wait, let me rephrase that to make it perfe...

"MOM! My show's over! Will you play Hot Wheels with me?"

Kristi Wallace Knight lives in Portland, Oregon, where she has been writing dangerously since 2000. She is currently the fiction editor for Stealing Time Magazine, *and is working on a novel about dragons and family.*

Sometimes Found-Wisdom Is Green and Slimy

By S. B. Elliott

As a break from blogging, I wrote a long memoir about my experience as an Army wife. I want you to feel my isolation and fear, and to know there are better and more effective ways of supporting our soldiers and their spouses. And I am in the process of writing my second book: a book of personal wisdom, and where I earned mine. There are so many ironies, so many brave coincidences, so many momentous pauses to record.

I write to inspire and support people who are in the process of finding themselves and embracing personal well-being. Interpersonal well-being. Community well-being. These are the people who will change the world. I also write because I find it nearly impossible *not* to tell funny stories on myself. Like the day I tried a homemade hot-oil treatment on my hair. Do you have any idea how many shampoos it takes to get a half-cup of hot coconut oil out of your hair? Mixed with powdered nutritional herbs? Three weeks later, the bathtub still had a sheen of gritty green slime.

A radiant experience, another ironic mistake, a personal challenge I'm working to overcome, or an ah-ha moment that enriched the way I view the world—even some tiny piece of the world. I hope that sharing my story will also share the opportunity for life-shift to occur. Mostly, this means that I blog. Blogging has the advantage of being mostly free and mostly instantaneous. Plus there's less pressure to intensively edit a blog before you publish.

I write with the intention of connecting to community. Reminding folks that we're all human on the inside. Integrating who I am with what I've experienced. And nurturing personal growth in myself and others. Compassion, humor and *joie de vivre*, authentically packaged with a gritty green slimy sheen.

S.B. Elliott is a Life Coach, Shamanic Healer and Reference Librarian. You can find her blog at SanctuaryWEST.org. When she's not healing clients' emotional wounds, offering lifeway workshops for well-being or hiking the Columbia Gorge, you can find her sitting under a cat, balancing her laptop on one knee and blowing fur off the keyboard.

Cynicism
By Gina Ochsner

If allowed free reign, the cynical eye roams hither and yon finding fault with everything. This petulance, the critical posture, the dissatisfaction—both vague and in particular—over time bends the vision, distorting the ability to see clearly, accurately, objectively. If I allow cynicism to drum with the heavy hammers of *"no good, no good"* against the tympanic membrane, I hear the winter wren in the dark hemlock behind our house. I can't recognize the beauty of its song nor appreciate the fact that the smallest, plainest birds compose the sweetest songs built of notes and shifting patterns and rhythms that seem to never repeat. I can't see what's out the window because my gaze has turned inside myself where there's nothing to behold except a vast and ever-widening chasm of fear.

A few weeks ago at a wrestling tournament I watched a boy from the local mat club wrestling with an opponent who was in the same weight class, but whose body seemed composed entirely of arms and legs. They were at a stalemate, 0-0 for the first round. At the start of the second round, Kevin, the shorter boy, assumed the down position on his hands and knees. The referee signaled the start, and for the next ninety seconds, I watched Kevin struggling to free himself from this taller boy who was now draped over his back like a human blanket. Nothing Kevin did seemed to help. In fact, the more he struggled, the more weary he became, and at one point the blanket-boy had Kevin folded up like a fortune cookie. I looked at Kevin's coach thinking, *Oh, boy, this is it. Kevin's a goner.* Instead the coach slapped the mat and shouted: "Good position! Now, get your feet underneath you, lean back and pop out! Up and out, buddy! Up and out!"

I had a minor ah-ha moment. Everything the coach said could be directly applied to combating my cynicism and doubt. If I could remember to keep my feet underneath me, lift my gaze up and out, I might break free. With my gaze redirected to the external I wouldn't be able contemplate myself, the appalling lacks and flaws and the huge valley of doubt I carry within me. With my gaze turned up and out I could then see others. With renewed purpose and humility I might realize that none of this—the writing, the living—is or was ever supposed to be about me.

And if my work—my life—is not about me, then I really don't need to worry about me, now do I? Now I am free to observe and consider anything and everything else. Oh, how liberating it is to crawl out from beneath the citadel of self.

"Cynicism" is an excerpt from "One Writer's Life," a lexicon of essays. Gina Ochsner lives in Keizer, Oregon, and divides her time between teaching at Corban

University and writing. She is the author of the short story collection The Necessary Grace to Fall, *which received the Flannery O'Connor Award for Short Fiction and the story collection* People I Wanted to Be. *Both books received the Oregon Book Award. Her novel* The Russian Dreambook of Colour and Flight *was long-listed for the Orange Award (UK).*

Gina is the grateful recipient of grants from the Oregon Arts Commission, Oregon Literary Arts Inc., The National Endowment for the Arts, the John Simon Guggenheim Memorial Foundation and the Howard Foundation.

Who

By Mary Milstead

For a long time, the characters in my fiction have been wild inventions. People fifty years my senior, a Mexican migrant farm worker, Bigfoot. Writing has always been a place for me to play, and a large part of the joy has been watching what these creations might do. I'm curious about everyone, and being a writer allows me to pretend like I'm entering other minds.

I wrote a whole series of stories about old married couples. Eventually I connected these stories to a cafe where I'd worked years before as a waitress, serving elderly residents of an apartment building who would come downstairs every day, for every meal. I think frequently about the woman with no teeth who ordered a steak every single night, cutting it into tiny slivers and refusing all attempts at conversation. She would just smile and wave me away. She's not a character in any of my stories but pieces of her are in everything.

I believe everyone we meet and all the stories we hear are fair game for writers. But mostly I'm an inventor, and I've spent years putting up a huge wall between my own personal narrative and the world of my fiction. Why is that? Is it because I'm afraid that all of my stories are secretly about me, anyway? Part of me that thinks I can protect myself as long as

I don't mine any details from my real life. Good old plausible deniability. I want to give a particular character a wide freckled neck, with freckles more red than brown, but I worry that my ex-boyfriend will recognize his neck. As if anyone has ever recognized his own neck.

Who are my stories about? Whoever appears when I sit down to write. All the people I've ever met. Myself.

Mary Milstead is a native Texan now happily settled in the beautiful wet Pacific Northwest. She studied at the Pinewood Table, attended the Tin House Summer Writers Workshop, and is currently pursuing an MFA in fiction at Portland State University. Her short fiction has been published in several journals, including The Portland Review *and* Konundrum Engine Literary Review. *Her novel is not really about Bigfoot.*

The Call of the Wild
By Martha Ragland

I write what is called commercial fiction, in this case cozy mysteries (picture Miss Marple). Working within a genre gives me pre-packaged structure and a story line. I like that.

I can still put into the book what matters to me. My sleuth is an elderly lady who once drove race cars for a living. This lets me write about aging and the passage of time. Why the race cars? I have no idea. I don't even drive fast.

To give my books verisimilitude, I volunteer at the local race track, where my ignorance makes me feel a bit awkward. If anyone asks what brings me to the track, I stumble on about re-creating Miss Marple, which can elicit mixed responses.

Yet the race track culture touches me deeply. Local tracks used to be a big deal. These days, the stands are almost empty. Volunteers—quiet heroes, I call them—still show up. They spot oil leaks, flag on-track dangers and dedicate themselves to keeping drivers safe. I've seen volunteers as old as I am stand ready to pull on fire-proof gloves, squeeze their no-longer-agile bodies through ragged holes in a chain link fence and run to extinguish an engine fire. "We're all addicted to speed," a volunteer sheepishly confessed.

I knew when I began my book I'd write about

getting old. Now I have another theme. Last Sunday, I attended a writers' workshop in the neighborhood of the track. When the races began, the sound of the big engines put me trackside. I imagined cars racing down the back straight, hurtling in a tight pack for the turns. I listened so intently that a home truth struck me: I too am addicted to speed. And to what I can only name the call of the wild.

Martha Ragland is a writer living in Portland, Oregon. She has published poems in Cloudbank *and essays in* Bark *and* Seasoned with Words. *In 2012, Mystery Writers of America awarded her one of two Helen McCloy Scholarships for Mystery Writing.*

It's All Right to Write and Not Publish

By Brian M. Biggs

During my college sophomore year I fell in love. Most college sophomores do. But this was a love that burrowed deep within my being. Clyde Hyke, a halfback on our football team, handed me Faulkner's *The Sound and the Fury* and said "Read this, you'll like it." Like it, I loved it. Not just the book but Faulkner, his words, his sentences, and how my mouth wrapped around those syllables when I read them aloud.

That's when I decided to be a writer.

In 1966, with a degree in theater, a Super 8 movie camera, and a Marine Corps uniform, I stepped onto Vietnam soil for a year-long tour of duty.

While in Vietnam I took a Creative Writing correspondence course from UC Berkeley and documented my work as a Civic Action Officer in the village of Hoa My (pronounced "Wah Me") with the writing assignments and Super 8 movies. This would be my book.

Marriage, three children and a job teaching high school theater put the book on hold. My writing took a dramatic leap to the plays we produced.

But when I retired in 1998 there were three trips back to Vietnam to reconnect with my Vietnamese friends in Hoa My, ten years of research and five years of reading chapters in a writers' group that produced a 500-page nonfiction memoir not yet published.

The money spent on trips, writers' conferences, editors, workshops and pencils could buy a Mercedes. But I entered a story from the book in a *Crab Orchard Review* contest. Second place! A published story. And a paycheck of $350.

At seventy I know that the older you are the longer it takes to live, but each day I find time to write.

Brian M. Biggs graduated from the University of Washington in 1964, where he majored in theater and played football (with a trip to the 1964 Rose Bowl). He spent four years in the Marines, including twelve months in Vietnam. Brian received his MFA in Directing from the University of Portland in 1974. He ran the theater program at Jefferson Performing Arts High School in Portland, Oregon, and for twenty-two years was Executive Director of Young Musicians & Artists, a resident visual and performing arts summer program held at Willamette University. He is currently writing, gardening and enjoying his wife's three horses on their five-acre ranch in Oregon City, Oregon. Please visit his blog at brianmbiggs.com.

What? Me? Well... Maybe!
By Gregg Townsley

I'm a Steinbeck guy, not a Hemingway guy, in large part because I began earnestly reading fiction only a couple of years ago. The literally thousands of volumes in my library are, to the point, nonfiction. And no, I haven't read them all, though you'd be surprised at how many I did.

Having now read the full corpus of a couple of contemporary novelists—Vonnegut, Hiaasen and Randy Wayne White to name a few—I find myself writing fiction, though reading doesn't qualify me to write. And even Vonnegut, though I've been amazed and entertained by him more than any other, doesn't come close to the artists, people tell me, that I've yet to read.

At work on my second novel, my first in the chute on Amazon with a third in the series planned for next spring, I'm surprised to hear my readers react, "You're just writing about yourself. This is you, isn't it?" So it goes.

I usually shake my head and say, "One only writes about what one knows," except that doesn't explain the similarities between my series' protagonist and the sixty years of Eric Hoffer-like adventures I've endured.

I write characters. The dialogue or events in their lives don't interest me as much. And I write in a place or time period I can enjoy or appreciate. I'm currently traveling in the 1880s, in Lake Tahoe, Carson City and Reno, as the explosive lode of gold and silver is beginning to decline on the Comstock. I'm having a ball. My characters' journeys are as amazing as mine.

I like the music in my head. And while I'd encourage writers to only write about what they know—here I should confess there have been a few sermons, pamphlets and term papers I've written that clearly don't qualify—a fun writer (I can't yet comment on what makes a good writer) has to let go to see where it's all going.

Like his character W. W. Ronin in East Jesus, Nevada *and the soon to be published* Lady of the Lake, *Gregg Edwards Townsley is a reflective, free-thinking ex-pastor and martial arts teacher living in St. Helens, Oregon, with his award-winning journalist wife, writer and muse, Nancy Lashbrook Townsley. His website and blog are at greggtownsley.com.*

Justification

By Dian Greenwood

Kate slices the huevos rancheros down the middle, dividing two eggs and black beans into equal portions. "I couldn't bear to stand in front of an audience and read my work," she says. Her hazel eyes hold the same earnest look, whether she's serious or laughing. "That is, if I should be lucky enough to be big-time published."

"I'd hate the stand-up thing myself," I say.

She hands me toast. "Good," she says. "At least I'm not alone."

"You're not." I sip my coffee. "Anyhow, that's not why I write."

"I wish I knew why I do," Kate says. "Seems so self-indulgent."

"I'm sure it looks that way. Maybe writing's a way to escape the world, to have time and space for yourself."

"Like running away from home?"

"Yes, like that," I say. "We climb inside our solitary caves and throw pictures up on the wall that we then record and eventually take to some conclusion."

"Like playing God or having ultimate control."

"Kind of. Except usually the story takes us where it wants to go."

"So, what's the justification for doing it?" she says.

"That's it," I say. "Writing's an excuse to sit, to read books, to huddle with other writers in some well- or poorly lit room where we share our stories. That's scary enough. As I see it, publication is justification for all that time and solitude. Otherwise, how would we ever explain it?"

Kate laughs. "Then it is self-indulgent."

"I wouldn't have it any other way."

At times, between Sturgis, South Dakota, and Portland, Oregon, Dian stopped over in San Diego and San Francisco where, after writing poetry for a few years, she wrote short stories and novels; The Yellow Cowboy Hat *is now in transit to New York. In her spare time, Dian is an avid moon watcher.*

The Writer as Creator
By Christi Krug

J.R.R. Tolkien described humans as "sub creators" who have been given the chance to fill "the crannies of the world." For my part, I've stocked the earth's crevices with manuscripts. I've fattened nearly a hundred notebooks. I love exploring the role of Creator, junior class.

This wasn't always the case. Twenty-some years ago, I would tear out any page of writing with a blot of imperfection. All my journals languished: empty.

Then I started magnifying the creating, not the failing.

I've learned that creativity doesn't demand perfection or require galactic power. God doesn't play it up as the most powerful entity in the universe, but as the most loving and vulnerable. As a mini-Creator, I embrace vulnerability.

Each time I reach for something new, I am raw, exposed. I have no idea what I'm doing.

My process builds on anything that makes me curious, enabling me to see the world in a new way. It is my gift, and also my challenge. I'm an octo-writer, waving tentacles in all directions. I write poetry, flash fiction, children's stories, fantasy, YA novels, memoir. I write how-to features and inspirational essays. I doodle comics and watercolor. If I were writing the same thing over and over, I might find a formula for success. Yet only when I am out of my depth do I plunge into awe.

A single life experience can produce endless surprises. For example, growing up in church got me writing for religious magazines. Years later, I penned memoir tales of my religious misadventures. A couple years ago, I came across a submission call for "Biblical horror." Why not? I thought, and now I write horror, too. Life keeps evolving, producing strange and unexpected things. Playing God is absolutely necessary, and indeed, it's all about play. Hand me that notebook, would you?

Christi Krug has won awards for her fiction, nonfiction and poetry. Her work has appeared in everything from neighborhood zines to worldwide publications. She is the creator of Wildfire Writing courses, and can be found teaching for Clark College or blogging at christikrug.net.

Interviews

Jon Bell:
Oregon Nonfiction

Jon Bell, a full-time freelance writer, turned his love of Mount Hood into a comprehensive book about the mountain. His journalism background shows in how he approaches his 11,245-foot subject from every conceivable angle, including on foot with his wife and dog.

On Mount Hood: A Biography of Oregon's Perilous Peak, was published by Sasquatch Books in 2011. It offers a satisfying mix of interviews and facts about one of the state's most recognizable features.

Jon takes the reader along on his quest to learn more about the iconic mountain that dominates the Portland metro-area landscape. His authorial voice —as he asks questions, delves into history and demystifies geological phenomena—is professional and personal. Well-muscled sentences push the reader to consider the peak's past, present and future and how its presence has affected us as human beings.

On Mount Hood is a relevant read for anyone who

has ever climbed Mount Hood, skied there, gasped at its immensity from the plane window, noted "The mountain's out today," or tasted tap water in the Portland metro area.

Jon, a former business writer for the *Portland Tribune*, has been freelancing since the late 1990s. His work has appeared in *Backpacker*, the *Oregonian*, *Oregon Business*, the *Portland* and *Puget Sound Business Journals*, *Oregon Coast*, the *Rowing News*, the *Home Building News* and the *Portland Physician Scribe*, among others.

1. Tell us about *On Mount Hood.*

Since the book came out in June 2011, I've had a lot of people ask me that. People often think it's strictly a history book or a climbing book or a natural sciences book. But it's really none of those—and all of those. Simply put, *On Mount Hood* is an anything and everything look at one of the Northwest's most famous mountains: adventures and tragedies, history and geology, people and places, trivia and lore. It's also a story of the mountain told through personal experiences, my own and those of countless other people, and a story that shows just how influential and inspirational the mountain is to people who live in the region or have otherwise crossed paths with Mount Hood.

2. What inspired you to create this book, Jon? How did writing it change your perception of the mountain?

There were a couple inspirations behind it, really. Mount Hood is just an inspirational mountain to begin with, especially for someone like me who grew up somewhere else and far away from grand mountains (Ohio). When I moved to Oregon in 1997, I was immediately smitten by the mountain, as so many people are, and started to explore it almost immediately through hiking, visiting Timberline Lodge, driving around it, camping near it and, eventually, climbing it. With the mountain so close to home, it's easy to make it a big part of what you do in your free time.

In 1999, I read a book called *The Measure of a Mountain* by Bruce Barcott, which is a narrative all about Mount Rainier. I loved it, and when I got to the end of it, I felt like I really knew a lot about the mountain, as if I'd read a biography about it. At the time, my wife suggested I write a book like that about Mount Hood, but back then I wasn't yet writing professionally, so I just sat on the idea for a few years while I built up my experience.

The idea never went away, and when I pulled it out of my head a few years ago, I was somewhat surprised but also glad to find that, aside from coffee table books, guidebooks, and a few fairly old books about the mountain, there wasn't a contemporary narrative out there about Mount Hood. So, I set out to write one.

Perception-wise, writing this book helped me not only get to know the mountain better, but to also realize how big of an impact it has on people and on the region in general. Mount Hood has literally changed the lives of people who have visited the mountain, fallen for it and never left. And so many people seem to have some kind of connection to the mountain, whether they've climbed it or skied on it, stayed at Timberline or even just heard about some of the climbing accidents while watching the news from across the country.

The mountain has such a rich history, and it's also connected to everything from the weather and the water to the trees. So for me, really realizing how far the mountain's reach goes was pretty eye-opening.

3. *On Mount Hood* is an enticing blend of facts, quotes and essay-like passages about your own climbing experiences. Where did you start, in terms of compiling information, and how many interviews did you conduct by the time the book was finished?

Over my years of exploring Mount Hood, and as a writer, I always kept pretty detailed journals of any excursions I made to the mountain. Because I spent so much time up there hiking and backpacking, cross-country skiing, climbing and just about everything else, I had a pretty good start when it came to personal anecdotes by the time I set out to write the book. As someone who always read about the mountain, I was familiar with a lot of the names of people who would make good interviews for the book, and once I started talking to people, every one of them would recommend at least a few other people to talk to.

The hardest part was having to put up some boundaries and just say, okay, I can't fit in any more stories for this chapter, even though I know they're out there. By the time I'd finished the book, I'd probably directly interviewed at least seventy-five people.

4. Was there one fact, anecdote or interview that surprised you the most?

There are so many that I came across, it's hard to narrow it down to just one. And I don't know that there was anything that really surprised me, other than the fact that so many people had so many unique connections to, or stories about, Mount Hood. Probably my favorite is that of Andrew Canfield, an Air Force pararescue jumper who was part of the 2002 rescue operation to help some climbers who'd been injured in a terrible accident on the South Side climbing route. He was in the helicopter that ended up crashing famously during the rescue attempt. Andrew himself was thrown from the helicopter and rolled over by it—twice—as it tumbled down the mountain. The fact that he lived to tell the tale is amazing enough, but his whole back story leading up to that incredible moment was fascinating as well.

5. After reading about Bull Run, which supplies the Portland metro area with water, and its vulnerability in the event of an eruption, I have to ask:

Did you rush out to buy a supply of bottled water?

Well, no, but it is interesting. Even though where I live now isn't supplied by the Bull Run, I did live in Portland for ten years and drank Bull Run water, which to me is some of the best tap water I've ever had. The watershed could be threatened if there was an eruption, but according to geologists I interviewed, such an eruption wouldn't happen without warning. The pipelines out near the watershed that bring the water into Portland have been buried underground as a safety measure, and the city does have a backup well field. So, knock on wood, the bases are hopefully covered.

6. Jon, you've been a successful freelance writer since 1999. What's the biggest challenge, or does it depend on the project? I'd love to hear about one of your most memorable assignments.

For me, the biggest challenge has always been related more to the business of full-time freelance writing and landing the next assignment or project that's going to keep me solidly busy and employed. It takes some real effort to make pitches, to market yourself, to get your name out there. And like a lot of writers, self-promotion and marketing is not really my strong suit, even though it needs to be. That's always a challenge.

My most memorable assignments are ones that usually come about as a result of something I'm out and about doing anyway. I love backpacking and climbing in the Cascades, so anytime I get to write about those kinds of excursions, I'm thrilled. I did a story once about climbing Mount Adams in a single day. It was fun and the experience itself was just rich with material. I got some nice photos, starting with a sunrise departure, the conditions were prime and on the 12,276-foot summit, just across from a group passing around a bottle of champagne, was a guitar and mandolin duo laying down a little bluegrass background music. Vignettes like that make for some great stories.

7. What advice would you give aspiring freelancers, especially in this economy, when there are a lot of creative professionals competing for the same kind of work?

Keep at it. Know that it takes a lot of work and time, but it can be done. I basically had to write my book—from proposal to finished manuscript—after hours, which wasn't always easy to do. It made for some long and quiet nights behind the computer when I would have rather been outside or doing something fun with my family, but in the end it really paid off, at least when it came to a real sense of accomplishment for a project that really was and is a passion of mine.

There's also a lot of change going on in the industry as the shift from print to digital continues, but I still think there's a good mix of both out there. I think there are a lot more avenues for new writers to pursue these days. Great writing will always be great, no matter the format. Finally, keep your writing balanced. I would love to write about climbing mountains or paddling lakes all the time, but that's not going to pay my bills. I do a lot of other writing that may not be as exciting but that is more lucrative. The key, though, is to be able to make a living but also to enjoy that living. So I always try to mix in the kinds of stories I love to do with the kind of writing I have to do. Striking the right balance helps put me right where I want to be.

Learn more about Jon Bell at his website, jbellink.com.

Scott Sparling:
Trains, Drugs and Literary Fiction

It's no wonder that critics and readers have praised Scott Sparling's debut novel, *Wire to Wire*. It's intense. It's provocative. It's also amazingly beautiful.

The heady pace of *Wire to Wire*, an adrenaline rush of a crime novel, matches the travel on its pages —by train, by Ford Ranchero and by tunneling us into the memories of protagonist Michael Slater. Scott spent more than twenty years crafting this book, and it seems as if the language itself is in motion, pulling readers forward into the next scene.

Tin House Books published *Wire to Wire* in June 2011. The novel received a coveted starred review from *Publishers Weekly* and was named a Pick of the Week. *Wire to Wire* won a Michigan Notable Book Award and has earned high praise from *Kirkus*, *Booklist*, the *Oregonian* and *Playboy*, among others.

Scott writes in a treehouse he built when his son was in elementary school.

"He didn't use it much, and I started taking my

laptop out there," Scott said. "It faces the woods, and when it's dark, it becomes kind of a blank space. I can sit up there and be anywhere. Sometimes I think Slater and the other characters are still living up there."

1. Tell us about *Wire to Wire*. What's it about?
Wire to Wire comes out of my love for Northern Michigan and freight trains, though emotionally it's about loyalty and love, and what happens when we get those things terribly wrong. It's sometimes called a literary crime novel, though I've never thought of it as that. It certainly has the elements of a crime novel, but they're taken apart and put back together in a weird way.

In more concrete terms, Michael Slater, the main character, falls in love with a woman who's thoroughly self-destructive, a woman who sniffs glue and who obviously can't love him back. There's a cost to all that, and it messes him up. So in that sense it's about how close we get to people and yet still feel alone at a very deep level.

The book starts with Slater working as a video editor, but seeing visions of his recent past play out on his editing screens. And what he sees is trouble. His car is stuffed with drug money and he's being chased by a killer. When he gets to Michigan, he falls in love with this damaged, seductive woman who is also his best friend's lover. Together, they get drawn into another dangerous scheme, masterminded by a local drug dealer who is kind of the puppet-master of this whole town.

That's the crime story part. And it's set in the fictional town of Wolverine, where everybody is damaged in some way—where sex, love, and money have just come off the rails. Though reading it now, I'm struck by how many chapters end with the character alone—on a train, or just staring at the screens, trying to make sense of it all.

2. Rave reviews. A book tour. A reading at the downtown Powell's. Since your debut novel was published by Tin House, you've earned a literary reputation that many of us have only dreamed of attaining. What's all the attention like? (Please feel free to gush.)

There's been a dream-come-true quality to it, without a doubt. And how often in your life do you get to say that and really mean it?

I remember getting a very short email from Tin House when they bought the book that said, "We all like *Wire to Wire*." The word "we" blew me away. More than one person had read it! Then I met them and was even more stunned—all these incredibly smart people asking me about my book. I am constantly reminding myself how lucky I am. There are a lot of great manuscripts out there that don't get the attention they deserve.

Outside of my family, nothing's been more important to me than this book, and when something gets that deep inside you, it pulls all kinds of levers.

At least it did for me.

Reading at Powell's was an amazing event. I'd worked most of my adult life to get up there, and when it finally happened, it was exactly what I'd hoped. I was just as stunned, in a different way, at a store in Petoskey, Michigan—McLean & Eakin. Only five or six people came to hear me, but they kept asking me about Harp and Slater and Lane. It became clear that the story had gone from my imagination into theirs. That floored me.

My ninety-one-year-old uncle came to my reading at the Michigan News Agency in Kalamazoo. He told Jaimy Gordon, who was also there, that *Wire to Wire* really wasn't his kind of book. So here's my elderly uncle and the National Book Award winner having this strange conversation about my book. Stuff like that is just unforgettable.

There's also part of the experience that's frustrating—mainly the marketing part. It's very hard to get the world to pay attention to anything for very long, especially a debut novel. But then I remind myself why we do this—we write for ourselves and out of loyalty to the stories we need to tell. Everything else is extra. I've already had way more attention than I ever thought I'd get, and I'm grateful for that.

3. *Wire to Wire* has two parallel tracks—Mike Slater's present-tense reality and what happened in his life three years ago. Those storylines are told from several characters' viewpoints. What were some of the challenges you solved to make that

unusual structure work so well? And how did you develop the concept of Slater watching his past onscreen while working in his editing booth? Did you plan that device or did it evolve as you wrote and revised?

I always imagined that Slater would be watching his past on the screens. I was inspired by that line from Jackson Browne's song "Fountain of Sorrow," where the narrator finds a picture of a former lover and sees the past romance differently: "What I was seeing wasn't what was happening at all." Some of that distancing happens for Slater. For most of the book he remains pretty haunted by the past.

Having these visions play on his editing screens caused two big problems. One concerned chronological time. I originally thought Slater's memories and visions should occur out of sequence, so that the reader would have the fun of reassembling them in the correct order. Slater has multiple screens in his edit suite, and sometimes I'd have one vision on screen two and another vision from a totally different time period on screen three. It all made sense to me, but it turned out not to be fun for readers. In fact it was pretty much unfathomable to everyone else.

I've seen books where that sort of thing works—*The English Patient* does it to an extent, and *The Book of Daniel* has some elements of that. But Ondaatje and Doctorow are geniuses. I didn't come anywhere close to pulling that off. So through eight or ten rewrites, I kept putting things back in chronological order. Each rewrite took six months, minimum, which is one reason the book took so long. It also means that early drafts are very different. A friend of mine showed me a manuscript I sent him in the early 1990s. There were story elements that now occur on page 300 or so in the very first chapter.

The other problem was the nature of the visions themselves. Are they real? Can other people see them on the screens? How is it that some of the visions on the screen show events where Slater wasn't present?

Tony Perez, my editor at Tin House, was immensely helpful on this issue—and a lot of other issues. In the end, we restructured things so you can read those scenes as playing on the screens, or simply as a third-person point of view shift.

Overall, Tony's comments and his ability to see the shape of the story greatly improved the book. I feel extremely lucky to have been able to work with him and everyone at Tin House. The entire experience—editing, book design, promotion—couldn't have been better.

4. Many of your scenes are bursting with physicality, especially your characters' in-the-moment experiences with drugs and sex. Do you have any advice on putting such intense physicality on the page?

I'm not sure I have any advice, other than reading a lot. I remember Robert Stone saying that the description of a fight is always more of a poem than prose, and that was useful to me. I think the same applies to sex. I also learned some things by watching how fight scenes are cut in movies—there's some purposeful confusion in the way action sequences are sometimes edited on the screen.

The early drafts focused mostly on trains. I wrote about freights in what I hoped was a powerful way. That was Harp's world. I wanted Lane's world to be equally vivid. That meant writing about glue and sex with equal intensity. I'm not sure exactly how it's done, which kind of scares me. A lot of it fell on the page when I was writing in my treehouse after dark.

5. Scott, I read in the *Oregonian* that you've been working on *Wire to Wire* for twenty years. Was there ever a time when you quit working on the book? Please mention some of the folks who encouraged you during that creative journey.

There were several periods when I put it aside and didn't work on it. I never thought of that as quitting, though—it was more just part of the process. Whatever else happened, I knew I was going to finish.

I completed the first draft in 1991. Two teachers —Jack Cady, and later, Joyce Thompson—were immensely important during that time. Joyce is the author of *Bones* and *East is West of Here*, and has a new book coming out next year.

My wife and I had a son in 1993, so my writing output dropped considerably then. By 1996, the manuscript was terribly tangled up, and I knew I needed to take some time off. For several years, I didn't work on the book much at all. I also took two years off, starting in 2006, to write a second book, which is half finished.

In 2002, I met Stevan Allred and Joanna Rose and started going to their weekly writing group, the Pinewood Table. I went once a week for five years and read every word of *Wire to Wire* aloud. I'd never met anyone like Stevan or Joanna—their commitment to and belief in fiction is incredible. They know how to talk about it in a way that expands your power instead of limiting it.

That table became like home for me. It was a powerful, almost spiritual thing because of the way they run the group. I also learned a tremendous amount from the other writers at the table. One of them, Sheila Hamilton, told me about Tin House and gave them the finished manuscript—that alone was hugely important, obviously.

The other factor that kept me going, honestly, was self-deception. Through most of the process, I thought I was just a year or two away from finishing. It was like a mirage that recedes as you drive toward it, except somehow I never realized that. I kept telling my family I was almost done. I remember one year I said I'd be done by Christmas, and my son Zane said, "Dad, just don't say that. It's not true, so don't even say that." I didn't believe him, but he was right.

Finally Stevan and Joanna just made me stop. It was a few steps shy of an intervention, I guess, but they made it clear I had to stop. I might still be rewriting otherwise.

6. You reference many songs and artists in *Wire to Wire*, and you have a wonderful playlist on your website. Do you listen to music when you write?

I used to have some Elvin Jones drum solos on a loop—not tribal drumming, but jazz drumming. I played drums when I was younger, and the rhythm of sentences is very important to me. The drum loop was energizing and it didn't distract me because it doesn't have a traditional melody.

Because I have a day job, I'd often write during lunch. If it was noisy, I'd put a song on repeat to create my own space—usually a sad song, something like Lucinda William's "Big Red Sun Blues." Anything kind of sad or lonely, played over and over, would work.

At home or in the treehouse, I wrote first drafts without music. When I was rewriting, I played Jesse Sykes and the Sweet Hereafter—every song she's ever recorded—over and over. It's trance-y and psychedelic and sad and seemed perfect for *Wire to Wire*. Toward the very end, I started playing Jon Dee Graham's album, "It's Not As Bad As It Looks," which shouldn't have worked because the songs are loud and so engaging. But it turned out to be great. Zane was a teenager by then, so maybe I was used to more noise.

7. What are you working on now?

I'm continuing to work on the book I started in

2006. Coming back to it, now that *Wire to Wire* is finished, has deepened my view of it. It's a book about brothers, and I don't have a brother, so I'm still finding out what that means to me. It's more tightly plotted than *Wire to Wire*, but the structure is just as weird, though a different kind of weird.

I haven't put much on paper yet, but I'm also beginning to work on a book set in Detroit. I haven't totally figured out if it's fiction or not—it's still in that exciting beginning stage.

Of course, what I've really been working on during the past four months is blogging. I've started a piece called "Adored, Ignored and Deplored," which is a satirical essay about the book tour. And I'm rewriting a few short stories.

And this piece, of course. Writing about *Wire to Wire* is always revealing to me—so thanks for the opportunity.

Check out scottsparling.net for more information about Scott and Wire to Wire. *Scott runs segerfile.com, an unofficial website about Bob Seger's music.*

Matt Love:
Independent Publisher,
Oregon Nonfiction

An intense appreciation for the state of Oregon guides Matt Love's writing and publishing endeavors. He's an original thinker, essayist and nonfiction author, and he founded the independent Nestucca Spit Press in 2003. Since then, he has published numerous, invaluable works on the state's culture, spirit and history.

Matt's latest book is *Sometimes a Great Movie: Paul Newman, Ken Kesey and the Filming of the Great Oregon Novel*, the final installment of his Newport Trilogy, which also includes *Super Sunday in Newport: Notes From My First Year in Town* and *Love & The Green Lady: Meditations on the Yaquina Bay Bridge, Oregon's Crown Jewel of Socialism*.

Matt is a tireless author and promoter. His drive to record stories rooted in Oregon is unparalleled, and he's committed not only to writing books, but to getting them in the hands of readers. Matt was awarded the Stewart H. Holbrook Literary Legacy Award in 2009 from Oregon Literary Arts to commemorate his achievements.

Besides the Newport Trilogy, Matt's recent books include *Gimme Refuge: The Education of a Caretaker; Citadel of the Spirit: Oregon's Sesquicentennial Anthology* (which he edited); and R*ed Hot and Rollin': A Retrospection of the Portland Trail Blazers' 1976-77 NBA Championship Season.* Nestucca Spit Press published Kim Cooper Findling's memoir, *Chance of Sun,* in 2011, and Matt plans to release a multimedia, tactile book by James Herman in 2013.

Matt is the Powell's Books "On Oregon" columnist and he writes "One Man's Beach" for *Oregon Coast Today.*

1. Tell us about *Sometimes a Great Movie.* What inspired you to write the book? What was it like tracking down information and anecdotes?

Not long after Ken Kesey died in 2001, I was in the Bayhaven, a bar on Newport's bayfront that was in the movie, and a man told me he witnessed a drunk Paul Newman come into a Toledo tavern one night during the filming of *Sometimes a Great Notion,* which was filmed in Lincoln County during the summer of 1970, and cut the legs off a pool table with a chainsaw. Finding out whether this incredible story was actually true was the guiding editorial mission of the book, and the story kept coming up over and over again every time I talked about it in public. Something did happen that night, and I figure it out by the end of the book.

In the summer of 2009, I staged a screening of the movie in Toledo, in a mill workers' union hall, and the place was jammed, the energy on fire like nothing I had experienced at an event. People shared their stories, brought in their photos and let me use everything. They put me on to dozens of leads. It just exploded from that night and I have to thank all the people who were there. They truly inspired me to write this book.

I interviewed more than a hundred people for the book and I never met anyone from Oregon who didn't want to share their experience. They were always candid, enthusiastic, and placed total trust in me in telling the larger story of the making of the movie. What struck me in our conversations, particularly with the key eight subjects, who became longer oral histories in the book, is how much they liked the Hollywood people and just hung around doing Oregon stuff together. There were virtually no walls between anyone that summer, and their resulting unique interactions truly fascinated me. Nothing like this could ever happen again—anywhere. And that warranted a book.

2. *Love & The Green Lady* **is the second volume of the Newport Trilogy. Why did you choose to feature the Yaquina Bay Bridge?**

I moved to Newport four years ago and began a

daily commute across the Yaquina Bay Bridge. Pretty quickly I had my whole aesthetic revolutionized by the experience and started taking all these photographs of the bridge while I was driving. I also started taking notes (while driving) and fairly soon, nonfiction stories connected to the bridge emerged, some of them mine, some of them historical, some of them from total strangers.

In the end I blended memoir, essay, vignette, autobiography, love note, letter, homework, meditation, ode, coffee table book, commentary, oral history, polemic, curriculum and confession and came up with something kind of weird, but so what?

There really isn't another bridge like this in Oregon, in its proximity to the ocean and the bay, its distinctive and eccentric art deco flourishes, such as the elegant green arch, beveled columns, obelisks, ornate railing and pedestrian plazas. All of these cool unique traits are the hallmark of Conde McCullough, the bridge's designer.

Basically I fell in love with the bridge and dubbed it the Green Lady because it seems like a woman to me. I've always loved great curves on women and the Yaquina Bay Bridge has them for sure.

Another thing I wanted to convey was how the Yaquina Bay Bridge has stood magnificently for seventy-five years as a monument to excellence in architecture and how a partnership between state and federal government in the throes of an economic calamity can produce something practical, beautiful and lasting. It is nothing less than an Oregon landmark and a powerful reminder how to build a great bridge. It needed a book, a personal book, a sexy book, not some turgid treatise.

3. You launched Nestucca Spit Press as a side project, and it has evolved into a dynamic publishing force—and a cultural authority—here in Oregon. What made you decide to start your own publishing company in 2003? How has the venture evolved in the past nine years?

Well, thanks for that kind assessment. The press has sold more than 12,000 books in Oregon, exclusively at events or through Oregon independent bookstores, and I'm pretty proud of that. We've all worked together to sell books and keep the traditional business of the community bookstore going.

I do think a couple of the books could have been huge regional hits, but I simply didn't and don't have the time or energy to seek distribution outside of Oregon. Writing books is easy—getting them distributed and into the hands of readers is the tough part. There may be a point soon where I really take the press regional, but I don't know how that would evolve. It's a little daunting to consider.

I started Nestucca Spit Press to get unique stories out: our legacy of publicly-owned beaches, the Vortex rock festival, the legendary 1977 Portland Trail Blazers' championship team, and I simply got tired of waiting around or listening to inane or indifferent comments by editors and agents. None of them really ever took the time to get to know me or what I was trying to do. They also never seemed to grasp that I was selling all these books by myself and understood the market. It was so absurd at times but I never let it block me. Doing this sort of thing with fiction is a lot tougher than the nonfiction books I've produced, but it's still doable. And the rewards of doing it yourself are enormous. I've learned so much and taken a lot of risks and have grown as a result.

It would be great to have a national book with a national audience to appreciate my passion for Oregon... but, if it happens, it will probably be a complete fluke. I don't worry about it any more and just keep writing.

4. Many writers have trouble with publicizing their work, but you're an amazing marketer and promoter, Matt. You have earned many fans by presenting entertaining readings, offering compelling facts and insights on panels, holding special events and getting community members involved and enthused about your books. What are some of the most important things a writer should do to publicize a new book?

The only real way I ever found success as a writer/publisher was to take the stories/books and my passion for them out to a reading public that was interested in Oregon. I've gigged at bars, barns, bookstores, galleries, coffee shops, theaters, utility closets, fairs, fields, parties, prisons, libraries, parks and historical museums. I have met thousands of

fantastic Oregonians who have responded enthusi-
astically to my personal, somewhat eccentric, approach to telling Oregon stories.

I put 320,000 miles on a truck—and never left the
state. I found my best readers at these events; I'm
closing in on 500 now since 2002. They could care less
about who or what published the book. They just
want to be engaged with the story or the passion of
the person presenting it.

Naturally, all writers/authors can't do this. My
fatigue from gigging nearly annihilated me a few
times. But you have to get off your ass and get out
there. And by that I also mean writing, writing everything you can, to get it in print and get feedback
from readers, and not just those in your writing
group. That's why I blog for Powell's, write regular
columns for several publications and keep a blog
myself. It's like training.

I don't hold myself out as a model. Other authors
have found success doing it differently or respond-
ing successfully (meaning e-books) to the various
challenges to the industry. I just know that if I hadn't
been willing to go out and meet librarians, bookstore
owners and museum directors, I would have never
sold more than a couple hundred books, and I wanted more readers than that.

**5. What are you writing right now? And what's
next for Nestucca Spit Press?**

I finished a novel about teaching high school
English. It's called *Teacher of the Year* and I can't really

classify it. It features diverse points of view, diatribes, letters, primary documents from the educational establishment, maxims, lesson plans, metafiction jumps, student writing, a paean to Lyndon Johnson (the only president who taught in a public school), graphics, an extra credit assignment and multiple equations for becoming a great teacher. We'll see what happens to it. Nestucca Spit Press won't bring this book out because I have larger aspirations for it.

I'm also working on a book about the rain. Not sure where it's going yet, but I like the way it makes me feel when I'm writing it.

I am incredibly excited about the next project for the press. In the spring of 2013 we'll be printing a short nonfiction book called *Driftwood Beach Forts of the Oregon Coast*. It's being put together by a young artist and writer named James Herman and it will feature photographs and James' wonderfully exquisite line drawings. This book is pure Oregon Coast and people will love it.

6. Your books are consistently political and personal. What motivates you to capture these important Oregon events, icons and experiences? Is there anyone doing anything like this in other states?

Oregon's progressive legacy, the internationally famous one established by Governor Tom McCall and a bipartisan legislature in the late 1960s and early 1970s, helped shape who I am today as a citizen, writer and teacher. All the great things that many associate with contemporary Oregon, like public beaches, bike paths, land use planning, etc., came out of McCall's two terms, which, by the way, I call the Stone Oregon Era. I feel a real responsibility to protect this legacy from the likes of idiots like Lars Larson. They want us to become like Houston.

I have often wondered if there is a writer/ publisher similar to me in other states. I don't know. Surely there is.

7. I was especially moved by your memoir, *Gimme Refuge: The Education of a Caretaker*. After penning many nonfiction books about Oregon and its rich history, what was it like to tell your own story? How has *Gimme Refuge* been received by your readers?

Gimme Refuge was a huge hit with teachers, and I received many incredible, personal emails and letters from teachers thanking me for writing an honest account of teaching. So often the profession is the victim of cliché (or loathing) in popular media. Most of the books written about teachers fall into one of three categories: 1) Hero teacher saves underprivileged minority children; 2) A dilettante non-teacher teaches for a year in a rough setting and shares his account; 3) Journalist hangs around a school for a year and writes a polemic about the terrible state of American education.

Gimme Refuge is nothing like that. It is about how and why people become teachers and what it costs to teach with (or without) purpose and passion.

I had initially billed the book as a nature memoir but I can see now it worked on many different levels. I rewrote the current version and added 15,000 words to it and I've entertained national aspirations for it. I've pitched it here and there and nothing's happened. Who knows? Maybe I'll put out this new version myself. Not sure at this point.

For more information about Matt and his publishing career, check out the Nestucca Spit Press website, nestuccaspitpress.com.

Michael Gettel-Gilmartin:
Middle Grade Fiction

With equal parts wit and hard work, middle grade author Michael Gettel-Gilmartin has built a loyal online presence.

His first blog, The Year of Writing Dangerously, sparked a spinoff site, Middle Grade Mafioso. Then Michael was invited to contribute to Project Mayhem: The Manic Minds of Middle Grade Writers. And then he joined Twitter. His thoughtful posts and tweets have paid off in a substantial readership.

Michael's completed novel, *Shakespeare on the Lam*, features Jared Hearne, a spunky, perceptive sixth-grader determined to figure out why mysterious things are happening in his Portland, Oregon, home. *Shakespeare on the Lam* tells the story of Jared's quest and what he learns along the way, using humor and action to explore family relationships, the middle-school social hierarchy and—of course—Shakespeare. Michael draws his characters deftly, delivering scenes and revelations with a close-in, casual voice that's a blend of cafeteria wisdom and age-appropriate wordplay.

It's the fun (and funny) page-turning kind of novel that encourages kids to stay up too late, reading by flashlight under their covers. And it's hard to believe that the story was written by anyone other than a sixth-grade boy.

Michael, the son of a British diplomat, has lived in eight countries. He is represented by Stephen Fraser at the Jennifer DeChiara Literary Agency.

1. What are you working on now?

I've written one and a half novels in 2012. The first I'm tentatively titling *The Friday Night Fright Club,* sort of a cross between *The Mother-Daughter Book Club* and *Goosebumps.* Three best friends, an interloper and a murderous ghost.

It's on furlough right now (i.e. sitting in a drawer waiting for my red pen of revision) because I immediately got inspired to write *The Comedy Wars,* in which the Muse of Comedy battles the forces who have stripped laughter from human life. (Percy Jackson, if Percy was a star on Comedy Central.) That's the half of a novel I mentioned. But working like a maniac takes my mind off being on submission. My agent since January this year, Stephen Fraser, is sending out my novel *Shakespeare on the Lam* to publishers.

I am so thankful to have finally found an agent.

Hats off to the mighty self-publishing brigade, but in my case I am a reluctant salesperson and probably couldn't sell a Girl Scout cookie if you paid me. I'd much rather be writing than doing business deals.

2. Why middle grade? What are some of the challenges of writing for this age group? How does middle grade differ from young adult, and have you always written middle grade?

When I started writing, many moons ago, I had no kids. I wrote adult fiction—a couple of humorous novels, and a couple of novels set in Japan, where I once lived, (one a "coming of age" and the other a P.I. mystery), all of them now safely trunked.

Then I had kids. I spent a lot of time reading to my kids. And I fell in love with the voices in middle grade fiction. Of course, the main challenge is one of authenticity, of remembering what it was like being a kid, and of not "writing down" to your audience.

As mentioned above, I really like humor. And middle grade fiction seems the perfect venue for that. As for the differences between MG and YA, I'll let agent Mary Kole (who writes the wonderful kidlit.com blog) tell it:

"MG books are shorter than YA, deal with any 'issues' or 'content' (edgy stuff) but only second-hand (like the kid's mom is an alcoholic, not the kid herself), have less darkness and often a sweeter ending than most books for older readers, are sophisticated but still accessible for reluctant readers, are more open to curriculum tie-ins and educational content, and are written to appeal to ten- to twelve-year-old readers, at their heart.

"YA books are longer, darker, edgier, less about education and more about a riveting story (though MG should have one, too, of course), and written to appeal to readers fourteen-plus."

3. How do you write? On the computer or long-hand? With a beverage or snack? With or without music? At a certain time of day? Do you jump right in or do you warm up with exercises or email?

I have written on everything from a typewriter to my spanking new laptop. When my oldest started preschool I went through a Starbucks phase, where I would write everything down longhand while eavesdropping on coffee drinkers. (Starbucks was way better than going home, where the laundry would call plaintively to me. Yes, even folding laundry was preferable to staring at the blank page/screen.)

I am a tea addict and drink gallons while writing. No snacking, or my waistline would be synonymous with urban sprawl. No music either, since dancing is the devil's playground. I'm a morning person, so once the kids are shipped off to school I launch myself at my manuscript.

I have a mantra of "A-Page-A-Day," which I have found highly successful. Daily writing means that it doesn't take me long to warm my engines. Just a quick read-through of the previous day's page, and I'm ready to roll. (When I'm revising, the page often gets completely rewritten.) Typically, I don't use exercises to warm up. I guess my fingers are lubed by my early morning email and blogging habit!

4. Michael, you are prolific blogger. Tell us about The Year of Writing Dangerously and Middle Grade Mafioso. Why did you start these blogs and what are your primary goals? Do you publish posts on a certain schedule—and if so, why?

I came late to blogging. My wife Marie is a blogger extraordinaire and for years I let her do all the heavy lifting. However, I kept seeing publishing types talking about "platform", and how to get one's name out there. So I took the plunge in early 2010.

The Year of Writing Dangerously was supposed to show how I continually pushed myself out of my comfort zone for a dazzling twelve-month span. However, I realized soon enough that I don't often stray from my tried-and-true routines. So I started to focus on reviewing craft books by such writers as James Scott Bell, Nancy Kress, and James N. Frey— as well as agents like Donald Maass and Noah Lukeman.

Middle Grade Mafioso started as a spoof after the furor about a possible "YA Mafia." I really just liked the blog name and didn't do anything with it, until someone found it on my Blogger profile, became a follower, and then prodded me with a "When are you going to get this blog off the ground?" I now use it mainly for middle grade book reviews.

I realized, eventually, that successful bloggers

write on a schedule. For Writing Dangerously, I post a "Monday Musing," which is really whatever takes my fancy; a "Craft Book of the Month" piece on Wednesdays; and something I call "Friday Fabulosity," which is usually a quote from a writer about their practice, and a short comment from me on what I think about it. For Middle Grade Mafioso, I post my book reviews on Mondays. I write each post the evening before publication.

My third blog, Project Mayhem, is a group blog founded by Hilary Wagner, author of *Nightshade City* and *The White Assassin*. Most of the writers are published, and it's a great site if you want to explore the magical world of middle grade. There are often writing tips, ruminations on reading and the occasional book review—which seems to be my forte. Each of the thirteen "Mayhemites" writes on average one post a month, which is definitely doable.

5. You're successful not just in getting folks to follow your blogs, but in actually creating a sense of community around them. Do you have any advice on how to engage readers to subscribe and comment regularly?

I think I've been lucky. I have a band of regular commenters, many of whom I found while being part of a now-defunct meme called "Microfiction Monday." I've also found that when I comment on others' blogs, they often return to comment on mine. I try very hard to reply to each comment, which keeps the conversation going. (This can be time-consuming, especially if I have to track down emails.)

Like everything worthwhile, blogging takes time. The more you put in, the more you get out. I also joined Twitter at the end of last year, and found there are several tweeters with whom I've hit it off. They are good for driving traffic blogward, as well as generally "chatting with."

The downside to all of this, of course, is that it can take over one's life, leaving little time for creativity. When school started this September—and my youngest started kindergarten—I decided to do what my friend Duncan Ellis advises, and turn off the Internet. Well, except for an hour a day—I don't think I could go completely cold turkey.

Oh, one final point: I try never to say anything negative or disparaging online. If I don't like a book I won't review it. If someone's going ballistic out in the blogosphere, I tend not to chime in.

6. Has blogging about writing, and reviewing craft books, changed the way you approach your fiction? If so, how?

By writing about craft, I have found myself becoming much more adept at technique. Writing is like any other activity: the mechanics can be learned, and the more you do it, the better you get. That's not to say, to use a musical analogy, that everybody can win the International Piano Competition (for writers, that would be the Pulitzer / Nobel). But there are a whole bunch of darned good piano players out there (and published writers, too).

7. You read a lot of middle-grade fiction. Please name a few of your favorite books and tell us why they inspire you.

My all-time favorite is *Charlotte's Web*. I can't get through that sucker without bawling.

I tend to like novels set in interesting places. (I was the son of a diplomat and got dragged all over the globe when young.) A recent find was *Words in the Dust* by Trent Reedy, about an Afghan girl with a cleft lip and palate. Reedy did an awesome job of "humanizing" Afghanistan for me. I love the writing of YA author Beth Kephart (*You Are My Only; Small Damages*.) I don't think she can write an uninteresting sentence. I am also a huge Harry Potter fan.

I guess what I'm confessing is that I read all over the map. But I have a particular soft spot for middle grade humor. I love Chris Rylander's *The Fourth Stall*, which is kind of a mafia spoof of middle school. Also, Maryrose Wood's novel about three children raised as wolves who are now being civilized in a grand manor in England. It's called *The Mysterious Howling*. It got to the point where I was thinking, "Why can't I write like that?" When I start marveling and feeling envious, I know I'm in good hands.

You can learn more about Michael Gettel-Gilmartin and his fiction at The Year of Writing Dangerously, theyearofwritingdangerously.blogspot.com, Middle Grade Mafioso, middlegrademafioso.blogspot.com, and Project Mayhem, project-middle-grade-mayhem.blogspot.com.

Duncan Ellis:
Speculative Fiction

Duncan Ellis multi-tasks with manuscripts. He has numerous novels in various stages of development including an epic science fiction trilogy.

His latest standalone novel, *A Turquoise Song*, is set in a future Portland. It features a confident, forthright voice and a world completely transformed by technological advances. Imaginative inventions and gadgets abound, but the quick-to-ignite plot drives the reader through the unfamiliar landscape and into the story itself, which explores identity, consciousness and what it means to be a member of a particular society. The world Duncan has put on the page is complete, well-articulated and entirely believable in relation to where today's society might be heading.

One of the ways Duncan motivates himself, and pushes forward on his drafts, is by participating in the beloved (and extremely popular) National Novel Writing Month each November. NaNo, as it's affectionately known, encourages authors to bust out 50,000-word first drafts in thirty days. Think of it as a month-long creative sprint. The 2011 event had more than 250,000 participants. Duncan was one of nearly 37,000 winners. *A Turquoise Song* had a final validated 80,752 words.

Duncan has completed NaNoWriMo eight times, which means he has written eight manuscripts with full plot arcs, including the trilogy. The 2004 event enticed him to write fiction for the first time in ten years, and he has been writing ever since.

Duncan, a United Kingdom native, resides in Portland, Oregon, which usually ranks tenth or eleventh in the world for regional word count during NaNo.

1. Tell us about your trilogy. And what's it like taking a full story, written in a month, and turning it into a more fleshed-out draft?

The original note I have for the story is that it is about a boy who becomes a king. The setting is a moon around a gas giant where human colonists have lost much of their technology—indeed, they have lived on this moon for so long that the very knowledge that they are colonists has been forgotten. As I was writing this story during NaNoWriMo, I realized it was a trilogy: the world was too big, and there was too much to say about it for just one book. It didn't hurt that the story naturally fell into three parts.

Still, reading that first précis draft after its regulation six weeks in a drawer was revelatory: there was so much I had written that I didn't remember writing. There were rough spots aplenty, but the good bits were so juicy and fresh. The process of populating the rest of the story to match that juiciness is thrilling—almost terrifying.

I have completed story arcs for all three books, and the first book is in roughly finished shape—an incomplete second draft, basically. The setting is pretty settled, and I am at the point of sharpening the narratives of the three main characters—trying to make it so that someone would actually care about the choices they make.

I will pick the draft up again in December and plan to finish it over the next year.

2. You started participating in NaNoWriMo eight years ago. What initially sparked your interest, and why have you continued to write a novel every November?

I was already a roundly frustrated writer in 2004. I have always harbored an ambition to write, but at that point I hadn't written any fiction in the best part of ten years. That was also the year I completed a marathon, so I was energized and looking for another challenge. I was pretty doubtful about knocking out a novel in only a month, though.

Chris Baty (the NaNoWriMo founder) was on a speaking tour for his book, *No Plot? No Problem!*, and

I thought I would go along and hear what he had to say. He's a very engaging speaker, and I left Powell's completely sold on the idea of writing a novel. I dusted off an old idea for a story that I had never got past chapter two with before, and blasted through the 50,000 in about three weeks. NaNoWriMo got me writing again.

I continue to participate mainly because November is the one time of the year when my writing comes first, and because high velocity noveling generates such compelling ideas. My goal these days is something north of 70,000, since I understand that the usual word count for a saleable novel is in the 70-80,000 range.

3. How do you make writing a priority in November, Duncan? Do you have a daily word count goal?

The nominal word count goal for the 50,000-word target is 1,667 words a day. I usually try to write a minimum of 2,000 words a day since I know there will be at least a few days when I will not write at all. That's about two hours of writing for me, as long as I have the plot broadly set beforehand.

I write first thing in the morning before the family is moving around, then at lunchtime, and on occasional special days during the month. Some years that has been Saturday mornings; one year I had enough spare vacation time to be able to take most Wednesdays off work.

None of this would be possible without my

wonderful wife. Fortunately she also happens to like to read what I write!

4. Have you found a sense of community here in Portland around NaNoWriMo? Has that community enriched or changed how you view your own work?

NaNoWriMo has a vigorous online community, which is great for providing support and procrastination opportunities. There are local chapters (so to speak) which are coordinated by a municipal liaison, and the word count for each participant is contributed toward the total for their region. I am always hoping that Portland will improve on its placing, but it seems to come in tenth or eleventh in the world every year.

During NaNo there are many opportunities to meet other writers: the kick-off event, regular write-ins (including the midnight write-in on Halloween to get folks moving as the clock ticks over into November—hurray for twenty-four-hour coffee shops!), and the Thank Goodness It's Over party to celebrate the achievement.

I've made some good friends through NaNoWriMo, but I am not in any critique groups at the moment.

5. Do you plot out your NaNo novels? If so, to what degree? Do you know where each scene is going or do you plan a world and then begin writing?

I can't write at five in the morning without some kind of plot to guide me.

I go into NaNo with descriptions for the main characters, chapter summaries and some notes on the world I'm writing in. I usually have around twenty-five chapters planned, the goal being to write at least 2,000 words in each chapter (which means I try to write a chapter a day). Each chapter's notes give a starting point, an ending point, the main characters involved and notes on things that need to happen. I leave location and incidental characters loose.

The biggest problem with this approach is that I end up introducing a lot of incidental details that appear exactly once, but then this is also where the best inventions come—and these things can be smoothed over in the revision process.

6. You are a veteran survivor of grueling writing days. How do you keep yourself fueled up and focused? Any tips for people working on tight deadlines?

Coffee. And tea. Lots of coffee and tea. Caffeinated beverages should account for somewhere between 96.9 and 97.3 percent of your fluids during November.

Actually, I drink a lot of water and exercise regularly, otherwise I get awfully jittery. During November that means cycling to work more, since my usual lunchtime run is preempted by the writing. But it really does help to stay on the exercise.

For the writing itself, there are three basic rules I follow:

▪ Never look back. You don't have time to edit as well as write during November, regardless of your opinions of revision of a draft in progress.

▪ Turn off the Internet. If there's something you need to check, put [a comment in square brackets] as a reminder when you do the revision. Losing an hour to in-depth research of whimsical cat pictures is death to word count.

▪ Don't delete anything. They are words you wrote, so they count towards your total for the month. Different people approach this differently: I [put unwanted words in square brackets], some people strike through the bad text, and still others have a morgue at the end of the document where they move surplus verbiage.

7. You mentioned you write the kinds of novels you love to read. Could you list a few of your favorite books or authors?

I read an awful lot of science fiction when I was growing up—the classic authors like Asimov, Clarke and Heinlein. And I am very sad that Douglas Adams didn't write more.

My favorite authors now are weighted toward the British, inevitably: Charles Stross, Terry Pratchett, Iain Banks and Neil Gaiman. I also like Neal Stephenson's work.

For more information about Duncan Ellis, see his website, dunx.org.

Crystal Wood:
Travel Writing

Crystal Wood explored two very different places for her travel books—Las Vegas, her hometown, and Oregon, her adopted state.

She took to the road to research and write *Backroads & Byways of Oregon: Drives, Day Trips & Weekend Excursions*, published by The Countryman Press in 2010. As if that weren't impressive enough, she did it as a new mom, often with her daughter (and the diaper bag) along for the ride.

Crystal coauthored *Las Vegas: Great Destinations* with Leah Koepp, also published by The Countryman Press in 2010.

In *Backroads & Byways*, Crystal maps out scenic loop tours in various regions of Oregon, grouping attractions in easy-to-navigate clusters. Her writing style is conversational, and her personality transforms this resource-rich material into a compelling cover-to-cover read about the state. Each chapter offers highlights, must-see sites and local flavor, followed by practical lists of accommodations, attractions and dining options. Evocative photos capture the landscape in crisp detail.

1. Tell us about your book, *Backroads & Byways of Oregon.*

Backroads & Byways of Oregon contains ten trips ranging from those that take an afternoon to those that take a weekend.

From the very beginning, my intent was to take travelers off the two main freeways (I-84 and I-5) without taking them too far out of the way from their final destination. So many folks see Oregon from these two highways but aren't sure they should venture away from the main routes. What's there to see? Can I do it and still make it to my destination in time? Special circumstances (age of fellow passengers, type of car, etc.) can present challenges as well.

I wrote *Backroads & Byways of Oregon* with many types of travelers in mind. Sometimes travel writers focus on their own likes. My goal was to appeal to as many hobbies and interests as possible. If one trip had interesting geological facts, an enigmatic Victorian home and the state's only carnivorous plant, I made sure the novice geologist, architect and botanist knew about it.

I also tried hard to describe without critiquing. If the motel had a John Wayne-themed room, I didn't knock it just because I don't enjoy it. The Western enthusiast knows the motel is there and to request the Rooster Cogburn suite.

2. You have an impressive public relations background and have done a lot of publicity oriented writing projects. How is travel writing different than, say, crafting press releases? How did your professional background inform the way you approached such a huge amount of material?

I have to say that for me it wasn't all too different. I was taught to write press releases by journalism professors. This included being brief and leaving the unnecessary and fluffy descriptive words out of the release. Then I left college for the real world and every client wanted fluff.

In PR, the publicist has to find a balance between two very different worlds. The media wants releases with as little character as possible. I mean they read loads of them. Why not give them the info they need in a succinct and concise release? They'll be grateful and you'll earn their trust and respect. But the clients are paying you. They're paying for you to accomplish for them (with media hits) and they like their stuff pretty. And it doesn't matter if it's a group of oncologists or an RV show, they all think more is better. Very frustrating.

To write both books, I got to use my own balance of adverbs and adjectives versus factual writing. I can only describe Anthony Lake and Gunsight Mountain in eastern Oregon so many ways. The reader is already interested in—or traveling to— Oregon.

3. You wrote another travel guidebook, *Las Vegas: Great Destinations*, with Leah Koepp. What was it like writing about your childhood hometown versus writing about your adopted state?

It was vastly different compared to writing about Oregon. I wrote with the security of knowing that I knew one of the most infamous cities in the country like only a few folks do.

In 1973, we moved to Las Vegas. My mom was a blackjack dealer when women dealing at any of the casinos on Las Vegas Boulevard (The Strip) were still a new concept. My stepfather was a professional musician with some big names at that time. My childhood gave me an unusual vantage point. I not only watched the city grow but also noticed the deeper changes first-hand. Most every large city in America has changed over the generations, but there's only one Las Vegas.

For the Las Vegas book I was a witness, but for the Oregon book, I was an explorer. I love both, but I wrote about Oregon to let readers know what fantastic places, history and beauty are here. I wrote about Las Vegas not only to show visitors how to enjoy such an odd place, but also to defend my hometown.

4. You did much of your research when your daughter was really young. What was it like plotting routes and visiting communities while caring for a sweet little passenger? Do you have any tips to offer new moms who are embarking on professional writing projects?

While I was traveling and writing the books, I thought, "This is hard." Then later, when it was all done, I looked back and thought, "Wow, that was really, really hard."

It added another dynamic to writing that I don't recommend. It burnt me out quickly, researching and writing two books while caring for a baby. I have no family nearby and my husband's work schedule made it so he was unable to help much.

My advice to any other new moms thinking of doing something similar is to ask for help from other moms and from friends who are able to. One friend was unemployed at the time and loves little ones. It was so helpful to have her come on a trip with me. She even took notes while I rattled them off as we drove. Her notes were the best I had for the entire book. That being said, I am proud that I did it and I have some lovely memories.

5. What was the most unexpected, or the most unusual, place you visited while researching the Oregon book? Why?

That is so hard to pinpoint. I was surprised or amazed on each trip. Either I came across something I wasn't expecting, or the spot was even better than I thought it would be. The best I can do is list a few favorites:

• **The Oregon Trail Museum** (east of Baker City) most definitely pleasantly surprised me. The opening exhibit uses life-sized mannequins in a giant diorama similar to those many of us made in elementary school, except these have recorded dialogue about the hardships on the trail. Talk about hokey. But right after that section, the museum really takes the time and effort to teach every age about the experience of those on the trail. I learned about what provisions were taken and how they were packed in such tiny wagons. The stoves designed just for the wagons ended up being useless purchases and were found abandoned along the route. I also didn't expect to be so impressed with looking at actual ruts made by the wagons in the dirt around the museum. I left there with a much better appreciation of those who traversed the trail.

• **Three Pools** located in Opal Creek Wilderness (off Highway 22) was not only astoundingly beautiful but also easy to access. So many travelers just assume it's a long and difficult trek to the amazing spots, and this one is just a simple walk from a parking lot. Granted, the lot is twenty-three miles from the highway, but it's so worth it.

• At **Shore Acres State Park**, there's an impressive glass-enclosed observation deck for winter storm watching. But even more surprising is a group called Shoreline Education Awareness. These volunteers hang out in the park at Seal Lion Lookout, between Memorial and Labor Day weekends, sharing their vast knowledge of the area's animal life and flora to anyone who'll listen. They set up telescopes for a better view and are more than happy to answer questions. An unexpected tour guide!

6. In your many travels, what did you learn about Oregon and Oregonians? Anything you didn't know from living here for twelve years?

As I traveled for the book, I learned so much from Oregonians. In fact, I learned so much that I thanked them in the dedication. There's a quiet pride that Oregonians feel for their state. And because it isn't boisterous, there aren't a lot of outsiders who know how interesting our state is. However, I enjoy telling everyone about Oregon's fantastically interesting facts and history. Whenever I get the opportunity, I spread the word. I talk to folks visiting, new residents and those who have never put one foot in the state.

7. If you could go anywhere in the world, and have the chance to write about the experience, where would you go? Why?

I've written and erased the answer to this question multiple times. I'm horrible at choosing, especially from a list as vast as the entire world. Could someone else choose for me? As long as I have enough time to research, read and learn as much as I can before I go. Good Lord, I'd like to erase this answer too.

How about Sri Lanka?

Crystal Wood's books, Backroads & Byways of Oregon: Drives, Day Trips & Weekend Excursions, *and* Las Vegas: Great Destinations, *are available at Powell's Books or online.*

Stephen O'Donnell:
Figurative/Narrative Art

Stephen O'Donnell's figurative paintings make viewers feel as if they're peering into secret worlds. His is an alternative history, replete with charm and sumptuous costumes while still addressing modern sensibilities.

Stephen plays with gender roles as he creates lavish settings, often painting himself in elaborate women's dresses—and oh, the lifelike expressions he renders! Many times his work depicts a private reaction to a narrative that's right outside the frame, bringing a larger story-sense to each canvas. It seems as if Stephen's sharing the most beautiful joke in the world, and we've been invited to watch it unfold.

His work has been collected in the book *Gods and Foolish Grandeur: A Selection of Paintings*, which includes an essay on the *portrait historié*, a genre of painting he has adapted for use in his work.

Stephen writes about "life and the arts from a retrograde perspective" at Gods and Foolish

Grandeur, godsandfoolishgrandeur.blogspot.com.

His other blog, Starlight and Sweet Music: The Musings of Madeline Prévert, starlightandsweet music.blogspot.com, focuses on his 1930s performance persona.

In 2011, Artists Wanted, a New York artists' collective, awarded Stephen the top prize in its prestigious "Power of Self" self-portrait competition. The recipient receives "one year of your life paid for," a video documentary and a party.

1. Stephen, your paintings are elegant, formal and historic, and yet the moments you capture are impish and modern. How would you describe your original style to someone who isn't familiar with your work?

I think of myself as a genre painter. Like with classical genre painting, my pieces do capture a specific moment in time; something specific is happening when the image I visualize is frozen. Something dramatic—or not so dramatic. Since almost all my work is based on self-portrait, I'm the star of whatever little story is being told. I love embedding myself in a historic setting. I love working to get all the details right.

More often than not, I represent myself in women's costume. The female side of my personality is very developed, so it feels very natural to go with female costume—which is usually the most elaborate, the most picturesque. And it's also usually the most fun.

I think where my work differs from the majority of contemporary art and, honestly, from the vast majority of art in general, is that I'm not afraid to not take myself seriously. In telling the story, there's often a joke being told. Even if it's just the humor of a big, burly guy wearing the dainty attire of a French countess.

2. Last year, you won the prestigious "Power of Self" competition hosted by Artists Wanted. What has that honor meant to you, and how has it impacted your work and career?

It was a big surprise. I don't think of my work as really mainstream at all; I think of it as rather a niche product. So I was really surprised that out of all those artists, they chose me.

My career has been going very well in the last couple years, and I feel I've been inching forward to a place where I could begin to transition into being a full-time artist. The kind of work I do takes so much time to produce. So obviously the financial aspect of this prize has been a great step in that direction. I was able to go down to part-time at the day job, and the freedom that's allowed me has made a huge impact. Simply put: more paintings in a much shorter amount of time. Because no matter what else I need or want to do to further my career, it always comes down to making more art.

3. Why self portraiture? Has rendering yourself on canvas, in art, in a variety of classical settings

and poses—often in elaborate gowns—changed your view of yourself?

Right at the beginning of my career, I fell into self portraiture; it wasn't something I'd done at all up to that point. But once I opened that door, it just felt so natural. I've often talked about how I feel that using the self portrait takes away the trickiest part of portraiture: that the painting is about someone. If I'm painting myself, it's a lot easier to focus on what's actually going on in the painting. What story I'm telling or even what question I'm posing.

The historicism in my work, which is something I've mostly focused on in the last several years, is, more than anything for me, fun. I love immersing myself in those periods. I get to live a life in my paintings that isn't possible, was never possible. But in a way, these other lives that I represent are, in truth, so rooted in my personality, in my imagination—in the history of my imagination—that I think painting out these stories, these alternate me's, has probably made me a more integrated person. In my paintings, I can let all the different aspects of myself come out to play.

4. The level of detail you execute in each of your works is astounding. You render every strand of hair, every bit of lace and every jeweled embellishment with great care. Is that aesthetic inspired by your love of all things classical, or is it related to your drive to create a specific world within your art? Both? Neither?

The level of detail relates to two things. One, I'm kind of showing off. And I figure if I'm going to go to all the trouble to do all the research I do, and then come up with original designs for a diamond necklace or court gown or gilt table, something that would be perfectly recognizable to a French marquise circa 1785, say, I'm damn well going to make sure that the viewer can see all that.

But the other reason is that the particular style I have—really a lack of a painterly style—is so plain, in a way. I'm not able to just suggest detail. If I were a painter like John Singer Sargent or Giovanni Boldini, you would be able to see, with the flick of a brush stroke, or a daub of paint, the details that are all there, existing in the painting, even though they're often completely abstracted. My style requires that I spell it all out, describe all the detail plainly and accurately.

Also, partially because of the difficulties of working with acrylic paint, my paintings usually aren't very shadowy. They're pretty high-key. So everything is visible and has to be shown.

I think, in truth, my painting style isn't really classical at all. I'm self-taught, and I don't really paint like classical painters, so in a way I'm representing that classical world through a completely different lens. As much as possible, I try to make all the details I'm representing as accurate for that time and place but, in the end, I'm really creating a world that is only specific to me.

5. How much research goes into your paintings? Do you have any favorite history or art books that you use as references for costuming or settings?

So much research goes into each of my paintings. I want to get every period detail as accurate as I can make it. It doesn't matter to me if the viewer doesn't necessarily have the knowledge to respond to that accuracy. But that accuracy is very important to me. With the work I do, it would be very easy to slip into pastiche. And in looking back on earlier work, sometimes I feel that I didn't quite obtain, then, the level of accuracy that I would be able to achieve now. And so there's an ongoing self-education. I have so many books—history books and art books—and I'm constantly online looking for images that I can use as reference to design original costumes and furniture to use in my tableaux.

6. Tell us a little about your creative process. How do you begin a new piece—with an image in mind or a particular idea? When do you know a painting is finished?

It used to be that almost my entire creative process was done subconsciously. An image would appear in my head, and I would pretty much just paint what I saw there. Often now, I will come up with an idea for a painting that is suggested by some aspect of some old painting I see a reproduction of in a book or online. However an idea comes to me, there's always a moment of recognition that this is a painting; I can make this image in my head into a painting. The pictorial component is always what is there first. The meaning behind it is often only accessible after the work itself is done.

As for knowing when a painting is finished, it tells me when it's finished. I keep looking and looking for things that need to be worked on. Even after the work appears to be totally complete. Even after I've signed the piece. My eye is always attuned to the thing that isn't working, that isn't quite right. My eye is immediately drawn to that. So when the painting stops turning up things for me to look at, I know it's done.

7. Who are some of your favorite artists, and what do you love about their work?

Many of my favorite artists are painters that most people have never even heard of. A lot of them wouldn't be considered even very good artists. Much of what I get from them is instruction on how to make my work better. I can learn by their weaknesses and can be inspired by their moments of genius. The great masters can be a bit daunting. And so embedded in our consciousness that it's usually impossible to see them clearly.

Mostly the artists I love are the great portrait painters. Velasquez, Van Dyck, Quentin de la Tour, Vigée le Brun, Gerard, Winterhalter, Sargent, Serov.

Of the great masters, no one speaks to me more than Vermeer. His amazing immediacy easily transcends his iconic status; his "importance" and celebrity never cloud that for me. I love the perverse rigor of Bronzino and the Mannerists. I never cease to wonder at the variety and precision of the Dutch artists of the seventeenth century—still-life, landscape, portrait, genre, allegory—all of it just knocks me out. And Friedrich is probably the greatest poet of all painters; God and the unconscious are in all his work.

To see some of Stephen's paintings, or to learn more about him, check out stephenodonnellartist.com.

Sarah Cypher:
Literary Fiction, Manuscript Editing

For novelist Sarah Cypher, books are a passion and a full-time business. She's the editorial brains—and the businesswoman—behind the Threepenny Editor, which she founded in Portland in 2003.

Sarah edits manuscripts as a full-time job, using her keen sense of pacing, character and story arc to help others shape their writing. Besides manuscript critiques, the Threepenny Editor, a full-service editing firm, offers copyediting, query letter assistance and a range of pre-publication and design services geared toward self-publishing writers.

Sarah is an articulate spokesperson about the finer points of the craft, and her extensive knowledge plays out in the pages of her own novels. Her authoritative voice urges readers to submerse themselves in previously unimaginable situations.

The Idiot's Tale, a blend of literary fiction and magical realism, features a blue baby born to a Palestinian family in California.

In the still-in-progress *Room 100*, set in a post-apocalyptic Middle Eastern quarantine zone, Rabia, the protagonist, finds herself in a school for women whose students are plotting against the oppressive patriarchal police-state. The novel—speculative fiction that doubles as a socio-political thriller—is a fast-paced, intoxicating dance of political machinations and Rabia's internal reactions to those forces. The shaken, post-plague world comes alive through vividly rendered details and Rabia's increasingly uncertain relationships. She is surrounded by people who may or may not be trustworthy—or healthy.

In 2010, Sarah published *The Editor's Lexicon: Essential Writing Terms for Novelists*. It's a thoughtful, concise compendium of topics and definitions informed by her years as a professional editor. *The Editor's Lexicon* helps authors define unfamiliar terms, and dipping in at random can help with writer's block or with diagnosing problems in a work-in-progress.

1. You've been a freelance manuscript editor since 2003. Has your professional experience, and your familiarity with common writing pitfalls, changed the way you approach your own projects?

Being an editor taught me how to keep a comfortable distance from the page. Instead of letting story problems put me in a funk, I have learned to reread a messy chapter and say, "This is a typical first draft.

Good work. Now figure it out and try again." I've always tried to be respectful and helpful when working with other writers. It took a while to be that person for myself.

2. Tell us about your current work, *Room 100*— the basic story, the meaning of the title and where you are in the writing process.

The story features a school for women whose only requirement to graduate is to be chosen as a bride. The title refers to its central room, where graduating women cook a first meal for their husband; but a group of women occupies the room and begins protesting the social order.

Room 100 takes place forty years in the future, after a global disaster changes the political shape of the Middle East. It's about what would be different, and what elements of shame and struggle we might still see in a society that is recovering from more than a century of political interference from outside.

My protagonist is a young widowed mother who must make some unsavory compromises trying to get herself and her daughter to safety. Person-versus-society is an important conflict in my writing, which is why I'm drawn to speculative fiction. It allows the writer to look at big issues, but have some fun in the process.

I finished a draft of the novel in 2011 under a different title, but after having it edited by former Holt editor-in-chief Marjorie Braman, I've been working on some changes.

3. You devoted a year to research before officially starting the first draft of *Room 100*. Many writers shy away from that kind of grueling immersion in background material. What has worked for you in terms of discovering useful information and then keeping track of those details? Do you take notes? Make lists? Or do you keep everything in your super-organized brain?

I wish I had a super-organized brain! A semiorganized desk and piles of notes have sufficed, along with MindNode, a program for idea-mapping, to keep track of all the many parts of this novel. They're just tools, though—my process changes with every draft.

I needed the year of research just to feel confident that I could make up a world similar to the one we live in. I'm a little obsessed. For this novel, I started looked at suicide bombing. As a tactic, it did not originate in the Middle East, but the Israel–Palestine conflict, 9/11, and our two wars brought it into our social consciousness as something "incomprehensible," "evil" and "sociopathic." These words are used so often that they've congealed, and there is nothing a writer loves better than to stick her finger in the pudding and stir. I started reading and got interested in the puzzling case of women, whose gender roles in Arab culture, along with many case studies, taunt the conventional wisdom about who is a soldier and who is a terrorist. It forces some interesting questions, so the research was really just a continued experience of reading fascinating material.

4. Let's talk about your finished novel, *The Idiot's Tale*. What's it about, and why did you choose to tell this particular story?

It's a magical realist novel about the first grandchild to be born to an immigrant Palestinian family in America. Elspeth is born with blue skin, and resulting issues of her custody and care draw out her family's conflicts over their integration and acceptance. The story is about folklore, family, cycles of violence and, of course, identity.

Most of my family is Arab, very practical—and ten years ago I sort of ran away to Portland, Oregon, to be imaginative and artsy. But then I spent seven of those years trying to write an Arab-American realist novel, until I remembered that I only enjoy writing when I get to stretch my imagination. Hence the excursion into magical realism, and into a postulated future in *Room 100*.

5. Your work evokes a strong sense of place. Have you been to all the locations you write about? Please share a few tips on crafting vivid scenes.

Room 100 is set in an area that is loosely based on the Gaza Strip. It's difficult to enter Gaza—I'd need to be a journalist like Matt Rees. For the facts, I'm limited to research: I obsessively Google-Earth my locations, look at pictures and YouTube videos, rent films, read blogs, talk to my friends who grew up in the Middle East and check out books, current and historical, from the library. I'm also working on a second bachelor's degree in Arabic Language and Culture, and I have had access to some very helpful people through that.

I wish I could visit the futuristic land of *Room 100*, or the half-historical, half-fable village of *The Idiot's Tale*. But I will have to demur to Ursula LeGuin's answer in a similar vein: "I write about imaginary countries, alien societies on other planets, dragons, wizards, the Napa Valley in 22002. I know these things... I got my knowledge of them, as I got whatever knowledge I have of the hearts and minds of human beings, through imagination working on observation. Like any other novelist."

My tips are stock and trade for any other writer, too: use vivid, five-senses detail; consider your character's state of mind and point of view; and enter a scene as late as you can and get out as early as you can, before your reader remembers that she's a voyeur to your elaborate fantasy.

6. You're very goal-oriented and deadline-driven when it comes to editing others' work and writing your own novels. How do you stay on task? Has your athletic conditioning, and training for triathlons, influenced the efficient way you structure your writing life?

I learned that I need four things to stay sane: writing, exercise, paying work and goof-off time with the people I love. Over a period of years, I've also learned that any given day has room for only three of those things; but over a week's time, they need to be in equilibrium or I enter a funk and get nothing done at all.

Staying on task is usually simple. I worry a lot about keeping promises to people—whether the context is a client's project or a date night with my partner. I don't like to let people down, including myself. Conventional wisdom says that high expectations are unhealthy, but everyone is a little crazy, and this little bit of craziness makes overall sanity possible.

7. Writers spend many solitary hours hunkered over the computer, but when it comes to promoting our work, we're supposed to shed our over-caffeinated anonymity and turn into marketing geniuses. You're a great role model in terms of your strong presence on the web. How has blogging, tweeting and maintaining two websites helped you attract new editorial clients and/or market *The Editor's Lexicon* to a wider audience? Any tips for those of us who want to grow our online presence?

Shucks, thank you! I don't think of myself as being good at social networking, though. The Internet is a way of life for me now. I have lived in four cities in two years (my partner is in the military), and I've needed it to stay connected to my writing tribe in Portland. Making local friends is tough when you are already looking for a house in the next city.

As for social networking as a business activity, I found that publishing my writer's guide, *The Editor's Lexicon*, was one thing, but getting strangers to buy it cold—without the one-on-one rapport I get to build with potential clients—has been difficult. Kind words from Jeff Baker in the *Oregonian's* book section, however, correlated to a big sales boost, so I think unsolicited word-of-mouth praise helps.

The market is crowded, many good writers are publishing books and the Internet is populous and noisy. The biggest lesson I've learned is that people don't look; they glance. So I've tried to keep my business website small and clean, and write web copy that is simple, brief and speaks to a visitor's most likely reason for visiting.

A network helps build a platform of repeat visitors, and more important, an ethos of mutual aid. I'd recommend focusing time on building online relationships with highly connected people—like writing-related Twitter users with followers in the tens of thousands—and showing them that you offer valuable content. One tweet from @AdviceToWriters about my recent blog post, for instance, spiked my blog's traffic over one hundred percent for one day. That kind of momentum requires other people's help; you can't do it alone.

Sarah Cypher's website is sarahcypher.com, and the Threepenny Editor site is threepennyeditor.com.

Acknowledgements

Thank you to all the writers who agreed to participate in this project before it even had a name.

Gigi Little designed the perfect cover and logo for *Brave on the Page* and Forest Avenue Press. She has been an invaluable advocate and brainstorming partner throughout the publishing process.

Copy editors Nancy Townsley and Annie Denning Hille took such care with everyone's words.

Forrest, Polly and Alex, the Espresso Book Machine staff at Powell's Books, answered my many questions. Sarah Cypher shared her thoughts about small press publishing. Colin Farstad offered sage advice about putting together a collection and setting up readings. I've met many wonderful Oregon authors thanks to Tracy Stepp, the coordinator of HomeWord Bound, the literary fundraiser for Community Partners for Affordable Housing, which is held annually at the Tualatin Country Club. Steve Almond's self-publishing class at The Writer's Dojo helped shape this project in its earliest stages. My family supported this book in too many ways to list.

Stevan Allred and Joanna Rose, thank you for my tribe. Oregon became home when I joined the writers showing up at the Pinewood Table with fresh pages, all of us eager for you to nurture our work.

To be featured in a future volume of the Seven Questions Series, or to learn more about Forest Avenue Press, contact me through my website, laurastanfill.com.